"The combination of George Barna's incredible research and understanding of culture, combined with Jimmy Meyers's practical parenting and counseling insight makes *Fearless Parenting* a must-read. This book will give you great discernment in understanding how to parent a child growing up with today's cultural pressures."

—Jim Burns, PhD, president, HomeWord;
author of *Confident Parenting and Teaching Your Children Healthy Sexuality*

"*Fearless Parenting* is an important book to read, especially for parents of preteens, tweens, or teenagers. It had me questioning, wondering, examining, and even doubting at times. It also had me thinking about many critically important things that parents and professionals working with parents or teens should be concerned with. The combination of George Barna's research and Jimmy Myers's practical experience makes for a powerful one-two combination that blesses us as readers. This book challenges readers to examine their parenting reality and equips them with practical ways to effectively navigate their children through these difficult cultural waters."

—Mark Holmen, executive director of Faith at Home Ministries

"George Barna and Jimmy Myers are the perfect pair to write this book. They educate and guide parents to a more confident, graceful, and truly fearless way of parenting."

—Dr. Tim Clinton, president, American Association of Christian Counselors

FEARLESS PARENTING

How to Raise Faithful Kids in a **SECULAR CULTURE**

GEORGE BARNA
and JIMMY MYERS

BakerBooks

a division of Baker Publishing Group
Grand Rapids, Michigan

Published by Baker Books
a division of Baker Publishing Group
P.O. Box 6287, Grand Rapids, MI 49516-6287
www.bakerbooks.com

Printed in the United States of America

Library of Congress Cataloging-in-Publication Data
Names: Barna, George, author. | Myers, Jimmy, author.
Title: Fearless parenting : how to raise faithful kids in a secular culture / George Barna and Jimmy Myers.
Description: Grand Rapids, MI : Baker Books, a division of Baker Publishing Group, [2017] | Includes bibliographical references.
Identifiers: LCCN 2017004117 | ISBN 9780801000645 (pbk.)
Subjects: LCSH: Parenting—Religious aspects—Christianity. | Child rearing—Religious aspects—Christianity. | Christianity and culture. | Christian education of children.
Classification: LCC BV4529 .B367 2017 | DDC 248.8/45—dc23
LC record available at https://lccn.loc.gov/2017004117

Unless otherwise indicated, Scripture quotations are from the Holy Bible, New International Version®. NIV®. Copyright © 1973, 1978, 1984, 2011 by Biblica, Inc.™ Used by permission of Zondervan. All rights reserved worldwide. www.zondervan.com

Scripture quotations labeled KJV are from the King James Version of the Bible.

Scripture quotations labeled Message are from THE MESSAGE. Copyright © by Eugene H. Peterson 1993, 1994, 1995, 1996, 2000, 2001, 2002. Used by permission of NavPress. All rights reserved. Represented by Tyndale House Publishers, Inc.

Scripture quotations labeled NASB are from the New American Standard Bible®, copyright © 1960, 1962, 1963, 1968, 1971, 1972, 1973, 1975, 1977, 1995 by The Lockman Foundation. Used by permission. (www.Lockman.org)

Scripture quotations labeled NLT are from the *Holy Bible*, New Living Translation, copyright © 1996, 2004, 2015 by Tyndale House Foundation. Used by permission of Tyndale House Publishers, Inc., Carol Stream, Illinois 60188. All rights reserved.

The authors are represented by The FEDD Agency, Inc.

17 18 19 20 21 22 23   7 6 5 4 3 2 1

Contents

Before You Go Any Further   7

Introduction: *Fear Not*   11

1. The Need for Fearless Parents   21

2. Reject Fear-Based Parenting   39

3. Institute Preparation-Based Parenting   55

4. Taking Charge of Our Children's Spiritual
   Growth   69

5. Our Children Are Called to Stand Out   85

6. Prioritize Family Relationships   101

7. Reject Destructive Parental Behaviors: *Anger, Guilt,
   and Shame*   117

8. Reject Materialistic Entitlement   135

9. Rethinking Social Media and Smartphone Use   153

10. The Porn-Again Child   173

11. Parental Self-Worth and the Push   189

12. Consistent Application Will Enhance Your Parenting
    Experience   207

    Notes   219

Before You Go Any Further

This book has been written by a couple of guys with vastly different backgrounds and experience. One guy (George) is a researcher who spends his time collecting data and analyzing the statistical results of surveys and other forms of research. His training taught him to avoid drawing conclusions based solely or primarily on subjective interaction with a few individuals. The other guy (Jimmy) has been a youth minister and professional family and adolescent counselor for nearly three decades. He too spends his time collecting and analyzing data, but it is what George would call "soft data"—that is, dialogue rather than statistics, anecdotes and stories rather than frequencies and correlation coefficients. Jimmy's training demanded that he constantly draw and test conclusions based on the data he received from his counseling clients.

So this book has been crafted by two highly educated, professionally trained, well-respected men with decades of experience trying to understand people to help them optimize their lives. But as you can see, we approach that common objective quite differently. And that is precisely what moved us to explore working together on a book centered on a common passion.

How did it work out? Well, one of our most gratifying epiphanies has been that our respective experiences and wisdom add value to the other's work, creating a pleasing synergy. Perhaps even more important, each of us has learned new things from the other. And that truth raises our hope that you will also learn some useful lessons as you engage with the result of that journey, as represented in these pages.

Our goal is to provide you with practical advice to help you effectively influence the mind and heart of your child. Both of us have previously written books about parenting, but we believe this joint effort provides insights and handles on parenting that neither of us could have provided alone.

As you work through this book, we encourage you not to waste time trying to figure out which author is behind each story or revelation. But if you are too much of a sleuth to let it go, then the rule of thumb is this: if you're reading a counseling story, it's almost certainly from Jimmy's experience. If you're reading numbers or cultural analysis, it's most likely from George.

In the end, we believe it's not worth your time trying to disentangle who wrote what words or which guy came up with what suggestion. Whatever you read is contained in these pages because we both believe it. And in the end, all that matters is whether the information is of practical value to you. We are too old and have fought too many of life's battles to worry about who gets the credit or who stands in the spotlight. At this stage in our respective careers, we're just blessed to still be able to string together a bunch of words into a coherent sentence.

Our goal is to encourage and help you raise your children—particularly adolescents—in this extraordinarily challenging time. We are grateful for the opportunity to publish these lessons on parenting. Further, we appreciate your consideration of how the ideas described in this book can serve you and your family. Realize that we make no promises that anything we suggest will be easy or painless. All we can guarantee is that this is the wisest and best advice we know how to provide based on our combined sixty-plus years of observation, experience, research, and analysis.

A Statement about Confidentiality

Whenever conversations are mentioned between a therapist and a client, we have taken all reasonable steps to ensure the confidentiality of those conversations. In these vignettes, names, ages, the time frame of the conversations, and sometimes even the sex of the clients or respondents have been changed to protect their identities. Some of these subjects are based on an amalgamation of several clients who expressed similar feelings about a given topic.

Introduction

Fear Not

Robert and Martha were unlike most of my clients. They didn't really have any major issues with their daughter's behavior. Stacy was a high school senior heading to college the next year. They enlisted my help for the most innocent of reasons: they just wanted her to have someone to talk to about the future and her direction after high school. In fact, Stacy's behavior was so good that they really didn't even have to parent her much. She was such a well-behaved child that a curfew or harsh restrictions weren't needed. She surrounded herself with good friends, worked hard enough academically to earn good grades, and took care of herself physically.

Martha ended our session by saying, "We couldn't ask for a better young lady. She's a straight-A student and a starter on the volleyball team. She's also very active in the church's youth group, she loves the Lord, and she sings with the worship team on Sunday morning. We are so blessed she's not struggling with the things that plague so many of her peers." *My first impression was overly positive: great Christian parents, great Christian family, and I couldn't wait to meet this great Christian kid.*

When Stacy came to see me a few days later, I had to agree with her parents. She was bright, bubbly, well-spoken, and had a super personality. You could tell her faith was a real aspect of her life. I couldn't help but like her as we worked through the normal intake form that all the kids who come to our counseling center are required to fill out.

Toward the end of that assessment, the questions take on a more personal tone. That is often where we get a sense of the real person beneath the veneer. My interaction with Stacy went something like this:

"So have you ever been involved in any consensual sexual activity?"

"Yes."

"Intercourse?"

"Yes."

"With one partner or more than one partner?"

"More than one."

"What's a ballpark estimate?"

There was a slight hesitation as she pondered the question. "Oh, I don't know . . . six or seven, maybe."

"If you added oral sex, would there be more partners?"

"Ha, yeah, several more . . ."

"When was the last time you drank alcohol to the point of intoxication?"

"Last Saturday."

"How often would you say you drink to intoxication?"

"At least a couple of times a month. Maybe more. It depends."

"When was the last time you smoked weed?"

"Last night."

"How often would you say you smoke weed?"

"Gee, I don't know, a few times a week, I guess."

Stacy sat there, pleasant as could be, not the least bit thrown by my questions or embarrassed by her answers. You might expect me to have been surprised by her answers, given the angelic profile her parents painted of her, but after many years of counseling adolescents and their families, you learn to expect such inconsistencies.

Sadly, one common discovery is that the worldviews and daily actions of our Christian kids are not all that different from those of their "nonbelieving" counterparts. What sets Christian families apart from their neighbors is often spiritual cosmetics—superficial signs of their religion, like church attendance, Bible ownership, and using religious language—more than the existence of deeper, more substantive distinctives. The apostle Paul said that we, as believers, are to be a "peculiar people," but when we compare the actions and attitudes of families both inside and outside the Christian community, we're more similar than peculiar.

This account of Robert, Martha, and Stacy reflects the turbulence of our post-Christian era. We all saw it coming. We went from the no-holds-barred years of the '80s to the sky's-the-limit '90s to the solemn, fearful years after 9/11 to the Great Recession of the first decade of the twenty-first century and then to the highly individualistic era we now inhabit. Families never have been as lost, confused, and doubtful about the future as they are today. For the first time in the past century, a majority of Americans believe today's children will not experience as good a life as did their parents and grandparents. The sense of optimism and hope that has been a fundamental hallmark of American society has been replaced with fear and anxiety about who we are and what kind of life we may experience.

Parents feel as if they have gotten the short end of the stick. In counseling sessions, not a single day goes by that I don't have a heartfelt discussion with parents about how unprepared they feel to deal with their children's issues. In most cases, the issues they're facing didn't even exist just a few years ago. Parents are alarmed by what they see happening in their local schools, shocked by what passes for entertainment on their iPads, and bewildered by what their children are texting about after they are supposed to be asleep.

In such a rapidly changing society, without stable and widely embraced moral foundations, everything we believe and do is up for grabs. It seems as if nothing is certain anymore. This time of instability and experimentation has brought about both subtle and not-so-subtle changes in family life. Aspects of the Christian family experience that were once the exception have somehow become the accepted norm, as the story of Robert, Martha, and Stacy reveals.

After I speak about such matters in churches and at conferences around the country, a queue invariably forms at the foot of the stage afterward, where parents line up to ask the "expert" for some free but desperately desired advice.

"What if my son is doing _____?"

"What if my husband refuses to help?"

"What if I find _____ in my daughter's backpack?"

"My children don't know any other kids at their school who are Christian."

"I'm afraid of what my son will do if I take away his cell phone!"

The predictability of parents' questions doesn't make their emotional pain and fear any easier to address. They plead for an action plan guaranteed to deliver the results they have dreamed of seeing in their child's life.

"What can I do?"

"What should I do?"

"Where can I go?"

"What are my choices?"

"How should I confront him or her?"

A massive amount of uncertainty has caused well-meaning, highly educated Christian parents to question their own motives, actions, and purpose. And who can blame them? Consider the issues today's parents are confronting:

- Young people raised in Christian homes are rejecting their parents' Christian faith at an alarming pace.
- Minors are using illegal drugs at an all-time high rate (no pun intended).
- Texting nude selfies has transitioned from a fad to a rite of passage.
- Kids are downloading apps on their smartphones that expedite sexual hookups.
- Families are spending little time together, exacerbating the challenge of passing on the family's values and culture.
- New technologies continue to emerge that wow us intellectually while segregating family members from one

another and overwhelming kids with too much, too soon.

- Extracurricular activities demand children's attendance seven days a week, for hours at a time, often eliminating time that would be more profitably spent engaged with faith, family, and friends.
- Children from good homes have developed a grotesque sense of entitlement, demanding money, technology, entertainment, and more.
- The vast majority of Christian teen boys have viewed hardcore pornography online; many begin this life-altering habit as early as eleven years old.

Bob Dylan sang, "The times they are a-changin'." That lyric was intended to be hopeful and encouraging, but the changes we have witnessed in our culture and in our homes are anything *but* encouraging. In fact, they are downright scary. But we cannot lament these negative aspects of raising kids today without realizing that we, as Christian parents, have had a hand in bringing all of this about. In some ways, we have been our own worst enemies.

As we circle the wagons within our communities of faith, we often lose perspective. Do you realize that most people in America, despite calling themselves "Christian," do not consider Jesus Christ their Lord and Savior? Who is responsible for that? Statistically, the decline of the church in America began in earnest in the 1960s. The decline could have been reversed. In fact, the closer to the initial demise of the church, the easier that reversal would have been. Now, as the memory fades of a nation where biblical principles are the norm in discussions about public policy, parenting strategies, and even educational practices, turning back the rising tide of secularism becomes ever more difficult.

Parents today have a daunting challenge: rewire our cultural brains, starting with the minds of our children, to reclaim the Christian principles that made this a great nation. The role of parenting is perhaps more central than anything else in fostering that cultural about-face. Many of the problems faced by today's kids are facilitated by their parents in the home. Does that sound crazy? Then answer this: Who buys our young people the things that have seduced them into a life of materialism? Who buys them the smartphones that make naked selfies possible? Who is more insanely focused on youth sports than even the kids themselves? We each must take an honest look in the mirror and accept responsibility for our role in creating many of the tensions and snares that plague our families.

Is this a challenging time to be a parent? No question about it. Are parents today facing issues that would have been unthinkable to their grandparents' generation? Yep. But to paraphrase the words of a wise old man by the name of Mordecai, "Who knows but that God has raised you up for such a time as this?" (see Esther 4:14). Have you ever wondered why *you* are a Christian adult with children inhabiting the planet during this particular time in American history? Have you asked yourself why *you* are faced with critical parenting choices that other generations of Christian parents only had nightmares about? Have you had your moments of self-doubt, causing you to acknowledge you are overwhelmed and wonder if God made a mistake?

Our six decades of research, cultural engagement, biblical exposition, and family interaction lead us to believe not only that God has *not* made a mistake but also that this is all part of His grand plan for revealing His glory. In fact, *you* are a vital part of that grand plan. Nothing that exists at this moment has come to pass apart from God's permission. You are right where you are, married to the person you are, with the children you have, in the city where you live, in the church you attend . . . for such a time as this. You are not just a parent in this cultural context—you are a Christian called to parent your children today, during this most critical time in the church's history, because God the Father, in His infinite wisdom, chose to place you here at this time.

The apostle Paul explained your presence in this cultural minefield as that of "Christ's ambassadors, as though God were making his appeal through us" (2 Cor. 5:20). Realize that an ambassador is a representative serving on foreign soil. In other words, as Christ's ambassador, you are His representative in this place, at this time in history. He has specifically *called and equipped you* to be a parent right here, right now. You may feel overwhelmed, but the God of creation has faith in you to do His work in your home in ways that will impact the world. Who are you to doubt His wisdom, no matter how far-fetched it may feel?

When facing tremendous difficulties, fear may actually be an appropriate response. We're afraid for our kids, we're afraid of our spiritual ambivalence, we're anxious about the future of our country, we're afraid we will fail as parents, and we're scared to be seen as failing by others. But we must remember that *fear is the opposite of faith unless it is a healthy fear of God.*

You need not fear our culture anymore. In the pages that follow, you will be given the keys to be the light on a hill in the midst of darkness. Lofty words, yes, but not empty ones if you have faith the size of a grain of sand and commitment to be a servant of the living God. You serve a Father who can and will do all things through a remnant—the tiny, incapable, overmatched, underresourced minority of people who have sufficient trust in Him to do the impossible in His power.

It is true that if you keep doing the things you have been doing in raising your children, then the chances are good that the result will be inadequate. But it is also true that if you trust in the Lord with all your heart and allow Him to use you to facilitate His purposes, then miracles will occur. And our culture needs some miracles, doesn't it? Some of the most significant miracles needed are in relation to the next generation of Americans—the children God has placed under your command.

If you are a Christian parent, you are already our hero. By serving "in the trenches" of the spiritual battle, doing what you can every day to raise up the next Paul or Esther or Abraham or Deborah, you are changing the world. Loving God, your spouse, and your kids is a heroic task in the face of a culture that despises such commitment. But it is that love and commitment that will make a positive and lasting difference in this world. Your children are your legacy—your gift to God and the world. Through His guidance and empowerment, your family has the capacity and potential to significantly influence the world. Let's explore what we can do to prepare ourselves to be the cultural change agents He has called us to be—parents who raise children to love and live for Christ in ways that restore the kingdom of God on this earth.

He has raised you up for such a time as this.

1

The Need for Fearless Parents

For a decade and a half, my wife and I had at least one adolescent in the house. During one challenging seven-year stretch, we had three adolescent girls under our roof at the same time. Both adults and all three girls survived, although there were moments when the ultimate outcome was in question. In the midst of our parenting struggles, my wife and I learned a lot—about our children, each other, our faith, American culture, the church, and even the impact of our own upbringing.

Looking back on our experiences, and having analyzed dozens of national surveys that either I or other research firms have conducted during the past decade, it is easier to put it all in perspective now that my seemingly daily child-rearing crises are history.

The first decade and a half of the new millennium was not an easy time to raise godly children. Ever fewer parents took pride in their commitment to raising their children to be good citizens, godly people, and productive members of society. Instead, most parents simply tried to shield themselves from the blistering attacks they received from those who were intent on reshaping society's view of family, marriage, human development, identity, truth, and humanity.

Year after year, parents have been assaulted with an unrelenting barrage of insulting images and depictions of parents. That assault has been buttressed by a parallel stream of attacks on the traditional family launched by the liberal media, progressive politicians, and university faculty. Meanwhile, the rise of postmodernism—a self-centered, emotion- and experience-driven worldview that minimizes the role of God and denies the existence of moral absolutes—gave philosophical ballast to a hypersensitive, politically correct culture that cautioned parents against disciplining their children or exposing them to traditional ways of thinking. Adding to the chaos, the advertising industry aggressively used children as sexual objects to sell products and ideology, seemingly focused on destroying the remaining morsels of youthful innocence that MTV and the ACLU had not shredded in the previous decade.

Parents who sought to inculcate fundamental Judeo-Christian principles in the minds and hearts of their youngsters were ridiculed as backward, outdated, ignorant individuals guilty of passing on myths and fantasies that had been soundly discredited years ago. If said parents attempted to introduce traditional values and morals to their children, the guardians of progressive thinking attacked with a vengeance. The culture wars of the late twentieth century expanded to include an all-out battle for the souls of America's children.

22

Because of the direction our nation is headed, the pace of cultural change, and the significance of the transformations now in progress, the impact of parenting may be greater than ever. You would be hard-pressed to find a sociologist or family counselor who believes parenting will get easier in the coming years. In the "good old days," a husband and wife were excited to welcome a baby into the world and looked forward to sharing experiences and joys as their little one marched toward adulthood. Recent surveys, however, indicate that most young adults today are neither excited about having children nor confident in their own ability to prepare such children for the hardships the world will hurl their way. The declining childbearing rate in America, which has now reached the point at which women are not having enough children for the population to continue to grow, is one tangible reminder of how daunting it is to stare parenthood in the face these days.

Yet Americans often perform best under such pressure, rising to the challenge and producing amazing results. If you are a parent, or will soon be one, then we hope you will embrace the opportunity to add value and hope to American society by raising your children to be the embodiment of goodness and greatness. You have the capacity to do an outstanding job at this task; all that's in question is whether you will accept the challenge and invest yourself in the process until the task has been accomplished.

To give you some context, let me describe what life in America is possibly going to be like in 2030 unless you and millions of your peers step up and embrace that challenge. The year 2030 is little more than a decade from now, a time when most of the young children alive now will be in their teens or twenties and therefore largely imprinted with the substance of who they will be for life. Although what you are about to read is just one plausible portrait of America in the near future, this is a reasonable depiction of what we will likely face unless there are dramatic shifts in the trajectory of our culture between now and then—shifts that are likely only if today's parents accept the job of raising their children as their greatest gift to the world and perhaps their most significant service to God.

Maybe you're a bit hesitant to consider the future. We do, after all, live in a society that treasures "living in the moment." You may be thinking, *2030? That's more than a decade from now. I'm struggling to get through today, this week, this month. I cannot devote myself to thinking about what the world may be like that far down the road. Who cares about 2030?*

You should care, and here's why:

- If you have a child born anytime between 2007 and 2012, then 2030 is when they will likely be preparing to leave the nest and enter the "real world" of full-time employment, college, or some other form of independence.
- If you have children born between 2013 and 2022, they will be in their adolescent stage.
- If you give birth to any youngsters between 2023 and 2030, then those young people will be in their early, highly formative years before third grade.

What you do today, next month, a year from now, and even five years from now will imprint critical ideas, values, beliefs, and behaviors on your children that will dramatically influence who they become and how they live for the rest of their lives. Parents, teachers, relatives, pastors, community leaders, and other people who know and regularly interact with your children have an impact on them. *But nobody has greater potential to transform the lives of your children than you do.* You must exploit this opportunity; if you do not, others will fill that vacuum. To best take advantage of your God-given opportunity to intentionally and purposefully affect your children, it is imperative that you understand the times and know how to respond while your response can have maximum impact.

Keep in mind that the America I am about to describe is likely but not inevitable. If you read the description of what's coming and don't like it, the best way to avoid such conditions is to initiate the change—right now! To avoid living in such a society will require us to consistently and intentionally make substantial changes regarding how our three key institutions—family, church, and government—coexist. If you are a parent, in particular, you have a significant opportunity to alter the future through the way you raise your kids. As a follower of Jesus Christ, how you integrate your faith into your influence on the lives of your children will probably be your most important and enduring legacy. Make it count!

The Picture of America in 2030

I was raised in America when it was known as the land of plenty and a nation of hope and opportunity. Given its current course of development, however, that depiction of America will be merely a historical footnote to coming generations of young Americans.

In 2030, the United States will likely be wrestling with shortages of potable water and certain types of food. These deficiencies will not cripple the country, but they will upset the ability of certain regions to have consistent access to all basic resources. Shortages always affect the cost of living too.

Crime rates have risen significantly in recent years and are poised to continue to increase. Combating that rise will be difficult because the increases in theft, assault, rape, embezzlement, and substance abuse will be facilitated by a variety of social changes. Among those precipitating conditions are the revised moral code, increased illegal immigration, law enforcement challenges, and an overburdened and inefficient judicial system.

While millions of children will be born each year, a growing focus will be directed toward the tidal wave of senior citizens living in America. As Baby Boomers pass the traditional age of retirement and live longer due to improvements in nutrition and medical care, a greater share of the country's limited resources will be allocated to the needs of the elderly—often at the expense of the unique needs of twenty-first-century children.

The environment for raising children in the future will also be notably different from today's. Terrorism became a tangible reality for Americans in 2001 and has escalated over time. However, new forms of cyberterrorism will arise, and both chemical and biological terrorism are expected to become more common. Since 2008, our country's military preparedness has been drastically diminished while government funding was reallocated to social programming. The continuation of that philosophy will substantially reduce the military's capacity to effectively protect the American population, leaving the nation at risk and raising public anxiety. Meanwhile, the number of serious conflicts around the world will grow substantially, but the United States will be incapable of responding to them all. The world will be a more dangerous and unpredictable place in 2030. That will, of course, take a toll on the psyche of our children.

A major reason for the lack of greater investment in domestic and global strength—i.e., local police and military—will be the staggering national debt (which reached $20 trillion by the end of 2016), as well as the mind-boggling costs associated with repairing our nation's decrepit infrastructure.[1] Over the past quarter century, America has allowed its infrastructure to crumble, making only the "absolutely necessary" patches to get by. With government budgets already strained past the point of sanity, the nation's infrastructure will be in a state of emergency by 2030 unless our governance and funding priorities radically change. Watchdog groups will ruefully decry our ragged roads, thousands of unsafe bridges and tunnels, a power grid incapable of handling the daily demand, leaking waterways and insufficient dams and water walls, and widespread congestion that will snarl traffic and impair the environment. Politicians will routinely run from the cost of making the necessary repairs, which would be hundreds of billions, if not trillions, of dollars.

Emotional Instability

If you're wondering what any of this has to do with raising children, apart from the direct impact on their quality of life, consider the effects such an environment will have on their minds and emotions.

For instance, my generation (Baby Boomers) grew up intoxicated with the American Dream: work hard, exploit opportunities, get ahead, and enjoy a comfortable and secure lifestyle. We knew enough to relish America's freedoms and to understand they required us to serve the country as needed. The dream incorporated a belief in and a relationship with God, maintaining a satisfying marriage while raising our 2.5 children to maximize their potential, and pursuing a functional family experience for both present enjoyment and our children's well-being. We trusted their future would be even more outstanding than our own—that was part of our gift to them and had become an unspoken expectation from generation to generation.

The world in 2030 will instead feature the New Millennium Dream. We are already seeing this new dream get a firm grip on America; by 2030, it will have been in place for more than a decade. In this view of reality, the goal of life is to work enough to get by, unless your job is synonymous with your identity (in which case you will work constantly but enjoy it). The New Millennium Dream will include a belief in some spiritual being, but a view that all truth and wisdom come from within, not from that external force. Family will be considered solely a source of enjoyment, so choosing relationships like marriage will be uncommon because such a permanent commitment brings limitations and hardships after the initial period of happiness. A lynchpin of this version of the dream is that we get benefits without responsibilities: we are "entitled" to freedom, security, opportunities, and happiness by virtue of our citizenship. That energetic pursuit of everything we want includes a new moral code that essentially allows for anything—sexually, financially, relationally, ethically, spiritually—that delivers pleasure or satisfaction without regard to the long-term ramifications. Having multiple options to choose from will be expected, and being able to take advantage of a wide range of gratifying experiences will be crucial to our sense of wholeness and fairness.

The social conditions described earlier, experienced through the filter of the New Millennium Dream, mean that one way we will protect ourselves is by maintaining minimal confidence and trust in people and institutions. Sociologists will note the typical relational pattern to emerge: we start with a handful of close friendships that inevitably dissolve when a friend no longer meets our needs. Being the victim of such dismissal by others will push us to develop a thicker skin and lower our expectations of people, and lead us to make fewer commitments to others. The ultimate outcome is that we will become self-serving exploiters, viewing other people as a means to our personal ends.

The New Moral Code

Without the Bible or a dominant religious ideology to serve as the source of absolute truth, Americans will refine the current practice of basing their moral and ethical decisions on feelings. Personal experiences rather than convictions or principles will greatly influence our choices. We will esteem compromise for pragmatic reasons rather than consistent adherence to core values and beliefs.

The moral context in which our children are raised will continue to move them further from biblical principles. One of the most disturbing of the social trends they will experience is the dismissal of marriage as a sacred or necessary part of life. Cohabitation will be the norm, emerging as the new millennium substitute for traditional marriage. In fact, current data indicates that a traditional marriage (i.e., a man and a woman exchanging vows to stay united for life) will be experienced by fewer than one out of every three adults under the age of forty. Getting married in a church by a minister of the gospel will be viewed as quaint, a throwback to the old days.

With biblical marriage discarded as unceremoniously as last week's newspaper, other immoral pursuits will follow. A majority of children born will be welcomed into the world by parents who are not married to each other. The number of nonheterosexual unions will slowly and quietly increase. Sexual liaisons that occur apart from a commitment to marriage will gain widespread acceptance. A majority of Americans will embrace the idea of sex between two people who "love each other in the moment" as both logical and morally defensible. After all, they profess love and are living in the moment, two principles that will be cherished as foundational by the American public. Sexual liaisons among three (or more) partners will also be a more regular occurrence since such experiences will not transcend accepted moral boundaries and yet will offer the potential of temporary pleasure.

Further, without an understanding and a recognition of absolute moral truth—a concept that more than one out of every four Christian churches have already abandoned in their teaching and outreach—instances of lying and cheating will proliferate. Politicians have been engaging in these practices for years, with the media and voters seeking to bust them for their indiscretions. By 2030, through the inconspicuous prodding of entertainment and news media, we will be worn down to the point that we come to accept deceit as the norm and fight it only when it tangibly affects our personal best interests.

Because we will chase everything and anything that makes us feel good or delivers happiness and comfort, substance abuse will be rampant. Some will engage in alcohol and drugs to escape the harsh but unspoken realities of a life lived without God, purpose, and boundaries. Others will turn to harmful substances due to the mistaken belief that they will harmlessly provide the pleasure they desire. The well-researched tie between substance abuse and physical abuse will constantly be on public display, as cohabiting partners and their children, in particular, endure regular bouts of alcohol- or drug-fueled physical violence.

Marriage will not be the only traditional value to undergo a reversal of fortune in the coming years. By 2030, we can expect life itself to have less value in the eyes of most Americans. This is a natural result of a society in which feelings rule, the ends justify the means, and change is preferred to absolute or traditional principles. Abortion will be considered a personal and largely circumstantial choice, permitted by law and accessible through government-funded clinics. Poverty, as well as the deprivation, suffering, and deaths that result from it, will be widely bemoaned, personally ignored, and assumed to be a government responsibility. Suicide will be deemed a valid personal choice in an unpredictable, meaningless, and disappointing world. Naturally, euthanasia will be another acceptable option. After all, we will esteem having choices more than knowing or conforming to absolute moral truths.

Uncle Sam Steps It Up

Power loves a vacuum, so governments at the federal, state, county, and local levels will be sucking up as much power and authority as possible. Despite Americans increasingly distrusting government to do what's right or what is in the best interests of the people, the New Millennium Dream will lead us to acquiesce to the Great Government Power Grab in exchange for more and more "giveaways" that come our way. Government will create a constant flow of programs to provide goodies for the people in exchange for greater control over their money, property, and constitutional rights. The election of Donald Trump may serve as a temporary block-age to government bloat. However, given the international impulse toward socialism and government expansion, as well as the ideological pendulum swinging slowly toward the Left in America, it seems most probable that Trump's election may simply represent a short-term interruption of the Great Government Power Grab.

Consequently, the primary sector providing job growth will be the government arena. The act of governance itself will transition from reliance on the rule of law to a rule of elites who will rewrite the laws to their own liking. The American people, determined to work less, play more, and leave the thinking to elected officials and bureaucrats, will become startlingly dependent on the government for subsistence. While the masses will deny that America approves of socialism, an objective analysis of the situation will conclude that we have followed the unfortunate path of European nations that abandoned their freedoms in favor of government sovereignty.

The once-robust US economy will lose its vitality in the wake of government expansion, further dampening the enthusiasm of workers about career possibilities and reducing the probability of experiencing challenges and fulfillment from their vocation. Financial freedom will become a historical artifact as the government, especially at the federal level, encroaches on more and more sacred economic territory.

The economic quake will be facilitated by major changes in our public schools too. The shifts in educational content that began before the turn of the new millennium will accelerate in number and significance. Students will be expected to be proficient in Spanish as well as in English to ease our transition as a nation welcoming millions of immigrants from south of the border. Health classes will promote homosexuality and transgenderism as valid and equal choices as well as foster an understanding and acceptance of all forms of sexual behavior.

Public schools, which have long pretended that they do not teach values, will drop the pretense and launch an overt and aggressive values-education rampage. Abortion will be promoted as a means of retaining one's sexual and financial freedom. Severe punishments will be meted out to those who slander or oppose the rights of anyone who is feeling LGBTQ. (By 2030, the recent agitation about the inappropriateness of mixed-gender locker rooms or bathrooms will be lost in our collective memories; the government will have long ago outlawed such challenges to the government orthodoxy as hate speech.)

Christianity's role in world history will be rewritten as an aggressive and repressive faith that scarred the world. Studying Islamic and Buddhist teachings, positioned as examples of classic literature, will become mandatory assignments for all students; the Bible will be absent from those discussions and assignments. The only prayer allowed on school campuses will be among Muslim students who supply a prayer rug and a note from home. Graduation prayers of all kinds will be banned.

Religious Restrictions

The religious limitations experienced in the public schools will simply reflect the dramatic changes in religious expression and experience that will have redefined faith in America. Realizing the centrality of religious liberty to the freedom of the nation, in 2030, the "progressives" will be in the midst of a full-court press to remove Christianity from our lives, similar to what the Russians experienced during the godless reign of the Union Soviet Socialist Republics.

Christian churches will be fewer in number and more highly regulated. They will be held to a raft of laws concerning what they can and cannot do. Their preaching and educational content, as well as programming, budgeting, and personnel decisions, will be monitored and managed by new government agencies. Expository Bible teaching will be replaced by uplifting inspirational talks. Church staff will be a combination of believers and nonbelievers, as required by antidiscrimination laws. Church programs will be reduced in scope as budgets dwindle due to the elimination of the tax-exempt status of churches. Pastors won't protest these shifts too vigorously since their certification will come directly from the state and they will be approved for their particular placement by regulatory agencies.

Christian schools will be prohibited from teaching views that conflict with the prevailing principles of the state and the dominant perspectives of what the government defines to be scientific knowledge. In fact, the existence of such schools will be endangered by laws and public pressure to eliminate the teaching of "deplorable" beliefs and behavior to children. Even homeschooling, which has long had a tenuous degree of protection from government interference, will be scrutinized more closely than ever, with more stringent controls and limitations enforced by the government.

Public evangelism will be outlawed as hate speech and discriminatory. Families will be allowed to conduct religious discussions and practices in their own homes, protected by laws that allow for "freedom of worship," but such endeavors will be actively discouraged if they occur in the presence of multiple households (e.g., small groups, house churches).

You Determine the Future through Your Children

As someone who grew up in what might be deemed the golden years of America—extensive freedom, strong churches, the fearless practice of one's faith, voluminous economic opportunities, reasonably objective public school education, healthy families, acceptance of biblical truths as fundamental to justice and righteousness—this profile of the United States in 2030 is horrifying. If you had shown me that description and asked what country it described, the United States would not have been among the possibilities I considered.

But that is where we are headed, even if my timetable is off by a few years.

If this scenario comes to pass, which is certainly possible, it would be a massive understatement to say that life in the United States in 2030 will be radically different from the life that most Americans thirty or older experienced during their formative years.

And if this depiction of the coming America strikes you as "too political" in nature, perhaps you have underestimated the scope of the parenting enterprise. After all, parenting is not simply about serving as a guardrail against your child's potential derailment on the highway of life. It's perfectly normal to want to enjoy watching your progeny develop from a naïve and wholly dependent preschooler into a more reflective and experimental adolescent before emerging as a wise and independent adult. But to simply watch the developmental process transpire without parental involvement is not God's plan for you or your child.

Parenting is not a spectator sport; it is a full-contact, immersive commitment to honoring the God who breathed life and purpose into your child. Today that is a politically incorrect view of parenting. Your challenge is to figure out if you want to be either politically correct or biblically correct. The two options rarely put you on the same path of action.

Here's another politically incorrect reality. God warns us that our intimate involvement in the development of our children occurs in the context of war—an eternal spiritual battle—and we ought to be prepared to fight for our children's survival in the midst of that battle. He tells us that as long as we are willing to work with Him, we have no reason to fear the act of parenting. With God on your side, and His principles in your head and heart, not only can you win this battle, but you are likely to enjoy it too. Imagine, you can be a victorious and fearless parent!

That is what this book is all about. The year 2030 does not have to look like the environment described earlier. That is your choice. You can act out of fear and acquiesce to the ways of a floundering and godless world, or you can put God's ways into practice and fearlessly raise spiritual champions whose character and wisdom will prevent America from falling prey to radical secularism. Taking the latter approach will completely alter the course of history.

We chose to write this book because we have seen—through research, counseling, teaching, parenting, and personal experiences—that parenting matters! It may be the single most important task you take on in your entire life. Think about this: you are responsible for raising up a new person, introducing them to the basic principles of life, and helping them become a person who will positively influence the planet. That's a heck of a challenge and opportunity—and potential legacy. Children are, indeed, a gift from God (see Ps. 127:3), but so is the chance to mold their lives. The manner in which you do so can also be your gift back to Him.

The rest of this book will provide you with practical examples of how you can raise great kids—and get greater enjoyment and fulfillment from the process. We believe that a few tweaks in the thinking and commitment of Christian parents can facilitate a more positive and fearless parenting experience.

Trust us, it won't be easy. But if you can develop the insight and tools to succeed at raising great children, you will experience immense satisfaction from that journey. The pathway provided in the coming chapters will help you make the most of it.

2

Reject Fear-Based Parenting

Teresa sat in my office wanting to know my opinion of her taking her fourteen-year-old daughter, Kenzie, out of public middle school and homeschooling her for the remainder of her secondary years. She and her husband were contemplating the change due to the prevalence of vulgar language and inappropriate sexual expression by members of the student body. To quote Teresa, "Kenzie said that walking down the hall between classes sounded more like an R-rated movie than a place where children are supposed to learn. We've had it with that place, so we're going to get her out of there as quickly as possible."

I could certainly understand Teresa's concern, but this seemingly "Christian" response of protecting her child from these "dangerous and faith-destroying" secular teenagers struck me as knee-jerk and, ironically, sort of "unchristian." I asked her what she believed public school would look like if all the Christian parents felt this way and pulled all their Christian children out and safely tucked them away in a faith-based homeschool environment. Teresa thought about that for a bit and eventually had to concede that it would be a very bad place. I suggested that maybe there was divine purpose in this thoroughly discipled young believer being a student in this secular environment. Staying in that faith-challenging public school might be just where God wanted her to be, for His sake and His glory.

Let's go ahead and establish this right up front. I believe Scripture teaches that fear is the exact opposite of faith and that without faith it is impossible to please God (see Heb. 11:6). Fear erodes our faith. Fear is what made Peter sink when he got out of the boat to walk on water to Jesus, impulsively cut off the soldier's ear, deny he ever knew Jesus, and hide out in the upper room after the crucifixion. This is why the Word of God is so forceful when it comes to denouncing the spirit of fear. Read the following passages, especially the parts emphasized in italics, and see if you come to the same conclusion.

- This is my command—be strong and courageous! *Do not be afraid* or discouraged. For the LORD your God is with you wherever you go. (Josh. 1:9 NLT)
- *Fearing people* is a dangerous trap, but trusting the LORD means safety. (Prov. 29:25 NLT)
- The spirit you received does not make you *slaves, so that you live in fear again*; rather, the Spirit you received brought about your adoption to sonship. And by him we cry, "*Abba,* Father." (Rom. 8:15)
- But after he had considered this, an angel of the Lord appeared to him in a dream and said, "Joseph son of

David, *do not be afraid* to take Mary home as your wife, because what is conceived in her is from the Holy Spirit." (Matt. 1:20)

- One night the Lord spoke to Paul in a vision: "*Do not be afraid*; keep on speaking, do not be silent. For I am with you, and no one is going to attack and harm you, because I have many people in this city." (Acts 18:9–10)
- For God has not given us a *spirit of fear* and timidity, but of power, love, and self-discipline. (2 Tim. 1:7 NLT)

Despite this perspective, our research among theologically conservative parents of children and teenagers revealed that six out of ten (61 percent) admit to making parenting decisions based on fear. It is not just a strategy that doesn't work; it is disobedience to God.

From the time she was a small child, Kenzie had been vigorously trained in the Christian faith both at home and at church. She'd sat through so many sermons, Bible studies, and youth services that she had Bible knowledge running out her ears! Yet after all that training and study, both of her parents still *feared* their daughter's faith was going to fold like a cheap suit just because the kids in the hall were using bad words and exhibiting ungodly behavior! Kenzie's parents loved both God and their daughter so much that they were desperate to do the right thing. Unfortunately, we sometimes confuse the right thing with what appears to be the safest thing.

For many Christian parents today, it seems like the Lord is not their refuge and strength. They don't possess that peace that surpasses all human understanding. Many of us continue to live by sight rather than by faith and are therefore consumed by fear.

Listen, I certainly don't blame this sweet couple for doing what they think is best to protect their child and guard her faith. We've all made similarly motivated choices for our kids, haven't we? In fact, we've been doing this for a long, long time. This protective, fear-focused parenting style is nothing new at all. It didn't emerge with the advent of internet porn; no, fear has been the centerpiece of Christian parenting since at least the beginning of the last century.

This concept is so important that it ranks as the number one fundamental change today's Christian parents need to make. With church attendance falling and young adults fleeing the faith of their childhood by the millions, there is a desperate need for an essential change in the way parents view the spiritual challenges and growth of their children. Christian parents must stop allowing fear to be the driving force behind their parenting philosophy. That philosophy is both unbiblical and ineffective.

Instead, we would do well to focus on preparing children to take on this increasingly secular society and win the culture war. We must no longer protect and separate them from culture but prepare and train them to engage and ultimately transform culture. Long gone are the days when simply teaching our kids that Zacchaeus was a wee little man, carting them to and from Sunday school, then locking them inside the protection of our Christian homes are going to be sufficient for their spiritual survival. Like it or not—and we suspect few Christians would "like" the culture war on Facebook—our children will live the rest of their lives amid a dark, pervasive spiritual battle. If we love them, we will do our best to prepare them for this inescapable situation.

The Protective/Fear-Based Christian Parenting Strategy of the Past

As we spend the next few pages discussing fear-based parenting, understand that we are not suggesting that you allow your child to frequent the Shady Lady Lounge on Bourbon Street or that you pipe adult cable channels into your nursery. When children are young, it is completely appropriate to adopt a protective/preventative parenting strategy. Young children are at a distinct cognitive disadvantage. They do not have the ability to process the world around them in a "nonconcrete" way. Social, ethical, and spiritual nuances are lost on them; they are easily persuaded and therefore need to be protected from influences that may negatively impact their physical, emotional, psychological, social, and spiritual development.

But research tells us that by age thirteen, children have developed much of the personality and characteristics that will be with them throughout adulthood. So when our children enter those middle school years, we, as parents, need to begin moving away from this protective/preventative model. It served its purpose, sort of like kindergarten and elementary school. It has laid the groundwork for what lies ahead.

Here's a brief outline of this fear-based parenting style from the past:

1. Clearly identify and define the sin.
2. Demonize not only this sin but also the perpetrators of said sin.

3. Teach about the danger of being even in close proximity to this sin or these sinners.
4. Construct protective walls to separate our children from this sin and these sinners.
5. Feel pride that our children never participate in this sin or feel shame if they do.

I can picture a beaming Christian father, so gratified that he is sending his eighteen-year-old daughter off to Christian college unscathed by the secular, carnal world around her. He proudly proclaims to everyone at the graduation party, "I just want you to know that Lulu is the perfect Christian young woman. She has never been alone with a boy, much less kissed one. She has, of course, never seen an R-rated movie, never smelled the demon drink of alcohol, and wouldn't know a marijuana plant if it was growing right under her nose! How did her mom and I do it? What's our parenting secret that so pleases Christ and is the envy of everyone in our small group? Well, we've had her locked in the basement since she was ten years old. And as you can see, it's worked like a charm!" But that pride in our parental accomplishment is a tad misplaced, isn't it? If Lulu's never had the opportunity to make a sinful choice, that doesn't mean we have succeeded in teaching her to make godly choices. In fact, we've failed—and quite miserably. Why? Because we've failed to prepare her for life outside her home.

Our goal simply can't be for our children never to commit a sin while growing up. Since all have sinned and fallen short of the glory of God, that expectation would be both a refutation of the Bible and a recipe for parental disaster. Rather, our goal has to be to equip our children to love and honor God each time they leave our homes to swim in a sea of sin.

Have you ever heard of monasticism? In and around the sixth and seventh centuries, Christianity almost disappeared from Europe and the world. The last bastions of the Christian faith were the monasteries where the monks preserved this belief system and most of Western culture during a time of cultural retrogression and barbarian invasion. So Christianity was locked away behind thick fortress walls, and culture was left to fend for itself. That concept of seclusion from a radically secular culture didn't work then, and it certainly doesn't work now. In fact, my mom always used to tell me, "Satan loves the dark and Jesus loves the light." It's time we unlock the doors of our Christian fortresses and let some light in.

A Trip Down Christian Parenting Lane

For a people who, throughout Scripture, have been implored to "fear not," Christian parents have most often been petrified of the secular culture in which they have found themselves. In the 1920s, we barred our doors to prevent our teenage girls from becoming "flappers" who wore short skirts and listened to—wait for it—jazz! In the 1950s, we desperately attempted to keep our young people from viewing Elvis Presley's sexually suggestive gyrating hips—so much so that the *Ed Sullivan Show* broadcast him only from the waist up in 1956. And don't even mention the Beatles' long hair of the 1960s and living like hippies in the '70s, and who could forget backward masking, or backmasking, in the '80s. Okay, I can bet some of you are blankly staring at that last one. Look it up. Trust me, you won't be disappointed. The list, of

45

course, could be expanded for each decade. Each generation of Christian parents has felt the strong need to protect and segregate their children from the evils of a godless culture.

So let's recap. We've been fearfully protecting and segregating our kids from culture for decades, and presently, more of our young people are leaving Christianity than ever before in our nation's history. At this point, an old business axiom comes to mind that says, "If we keep doing the same thing the same way but expecting a different result, then . . . we're crazy!"

The Biblical-Based Parenting Approach to Sin

I once had a young man in my office who was struggling with same-sex attraction. He felt as though he was a huge disappointment to God. He was depressed and had been exiled from his youth group. And when I say exiled, I mean the youth minister had approached him and asked him not to come back until he had dealt with this sin in his life. He was told that his presence was too disruptive to the other students. It seems when word got out about his issue, several wonderful, godly parents had threatened not to let their precious children return to that church unless this offensive child was removed. So he was removed. There are words for people like that: the phrase "brood of vipers" comes to mind. Why many of us have chosen to model our faith after the Pharisees, those who stood against everything Jesus stood for, is hard to fathom. Segregation and judgment have never been the proper Christian response to sin. If we take an overarching view of the New Testament, I think we might find a more Christ-centered parental approach. It might look something like this.

Identify God's Behavioral Boundaries

We could begin by teaching our kids the joy of obedience. "Joy of obedience" sounds like an oxymoron, doesn't it? We should follow Christ's teachings not to avoid punishment but to experience the joy that comes from obedience. You know, obedience has really gotten a bad rap. When most of us think of obedience, we think of obligatory rules to follow or our dog learning to "sit." But the reality is that obedience is simply our opportunity to say thank You to Jesus for all He has done for us. Dozens of times a day we are given the chance to say thank You through the choices we make—choices that either please our Lord or pull us away from Him. Jesus put it this way in John 14:15: "If you love me, keep my commands."

Emphasize the Power of God, Not the Fear of Man

I have always been a big fan of Jesse. You remember him, right? He was David's father. I don't know all that went on in that house, but somewhere along the way, David learned great faith in the power of his heavenly Father. Somewhere in his young life, he learned to trust God rather than fear man and to run fearlessly onto the battlefield while all the grown soldiers were running away from it. And what did David say when he stood there facing down that giant Philistine?

> You come against me with sword and spear and javelin, but I come against you in the name of the LORD Almighty, the God of the armies of Israel, whom you have defied. This day the LORD will deliver you into my hands, and I'll strike you down and cut off your head. This very day I will give the carcasses of the Philistine army to the birds and the wild animals, and *the whole world will know that*

there is a God in Israel. All those gathered here will know
that it is not by sword or spear that the LORD *saves; for*
the battle is the LORD*'s,* and he will give all of you into
our hands. (1 Sam. 17:45–47, emphasis added)

Maintain Boundaries and Enforce Consequences

I guess God could have put an alligator-infested moat
around the tree containing the forbidden fruit to prevent
Adam and Eve from accessing it or placed GPS monitors on
their ankles so if they got too close He could throw Himself
between them and the tree. But He didn't. He simply told
them that they could not eat from it. They had every other
plant to consume to their heart's content, but not that one.
But did they obey? Nope. And when they did eat the fruit,
there were consequences. If you've ever witnessed childbirth
. . . well, you know what some of those consequences were.
God established clearly defined boundaries and lovingly enforced consequences when those boundaries were violated.
But did He ever attempt to prevent His children from sinning? No, He did not. The author of Hebrews does not say
that God prevents those He loves from sinning. He writes in
Hebrews 12:5–6, "My son, do not make light of the Lord's
discipline, and do not lose heart when he rebukes you, because the Lord disciplines the one he loves, and he chastens
everyone he accepts as his son."

Teach Our Children to Love Sinners More than They Hate Their Sin

I remember seeing a cartoon that had two televange-
lists standing in the middle of a barren, deserted street. It

was apparent that the rapture had occurred, all the believers had been taken up to heaven, and these two famous preachers were the only two left on earth. Everyone had been taken to heaven to meet the Lord—except them. One turned to the other and said, "I don't get it. We hated all the right people." You and I both know this isn't true, but we also must admit that this is exactly how many, if not most, non-Christians view us. We don't know exactly when it happened, but it was somewhere between Jesus loving everybody, the early church turning the first-century culture upside down by loving and taking care of orphans and widows, and today. Twenty-first-century Christians are known more for who and what we are against than who and what we are for. It's so odd. Today we are not known for loving people, which Jesus commanded us to do. We are known for judging people, which Jesus commanded us not to do.

This attitude is taught, first and foremost, in the home. As parents, in our zeal to keep our kids away from harm (which is important), we urge them to stay away from sinners (which is not a Christlike thing to do). Our kids unknowingly begin to equate repulsion of sin with repulsion of friends and classmates who commit those sins. And if we leave that thoroughly non-Christian point of view unchallenged, by the time they reach college age, they emerge from our homes as fully indoctrinated Pharisees. Contrast this attitude with that of our Lord when he saved the woman caught in adultery. John 8:10–11 states, "Jesus straightened up and asked her, 'Woman, where are they? Has no one condemned you?' 'No one, sir,' she said. 'Then neither do I condemn you,' Jesus declared. 'Go now and leave your life of sin.'" See, it's possible to take a hard line with sin while taking a compassionate line with the sinner.

Offer Total Love, Forgiveness, and Acceptance of People Regardless of Their Choices

In 2016, in his Tony Award acceptance speech, Lin-Manuel Miranda, the creator of the history-making Broadway hit *Hamilton*, stated that "love is love, is love, is love, is love . . ." Truer words were never spoken. Offering total love, forgiveness, and acceptance of people is a biblical truth. Many of us may give lip service to this truth yet deep down have trouble accepting it. *God loves everybody the same.* Let me repeat, God loves everybody the same. *Everybody.* He loved Pontius Pilate as much as He loved the apostle Peter; He loved Martin Luther as much as He loved Genghis Khan; He loves Kim Jong-un as much as He loves Rick Warren; and He loves the leader of ISIS as much as He loves . . . take a deep breath . . . Billy Graham. He also loves the drug dealer as much as the deacon, the prostitute as much as the preacher, and the sex trafficker as much as the Sunday school teacher. And if I'm not mistaken, we are called to love like God loves—the good and the bad, the sick and the healthy, the successful and the unsuccessful, the rich and the poor, the saint and the sinner.

We are to love people regardless of the choices they make. Besides, how can we judge other people just because they sin differently than we do? First Corinthians 13:1–3 states, "If I speak in the tongues of men or of angels, but do not have love, I am only a resounding gong or a clanging cymbal. If I have the gift of prophecy and can fathom all mysteries and all knowledge, and if I have a faith that can move mountains, but have not love, I am nothing. If I give all I possess to the poor and give over my body to hardship that I may boast, but do not have love, I gain nothing."

It is critical that we begin teaching our kids to stop being afraid of culture and to love and accept all their friends—the good ones as well as the ones who are struggling. But to do that, we, the grown-ups, must first do the same. In the words of Moses,

> Fix these words of mine in your hearts and minds; tie them as symbols on your hands and bind them on your foreheads. Teach them to your children, talking about them when you sit at home and when you walk along the road, when you lie down and when you get up. Write them on the doorframes of your houses and on your gates, so that your days and the days of your children may be many in the land the LORD swore to give your ancestors, as many as the days that the heavens are above the earth. (Deut. 11:18–21)

Our kids will learn nonjudgmental, unconditional love, not from the pastor, or their youth minister, but from us.

Remember the old axiom "You can't give what you don't have"? If you are filled with fear, you'll pass it on to your kids. If you're filled with love and forgiveness, watch them reflect those qualities in their own relationships.

Five Practical Changes You Can Make Today

1. Get with your spouse and honestly try to determine how much of your parenting strategy is based on fear. Then discuss ways to modify or change those strategies.

2. When you find out a friend of your child has been acting out and making harmful life choices, talk with your child about how they might help their friend and minister to them. Teach them to love their friend while holding fast to a more Christ-honoring way of living.

3. Every week, pray with your child specifically for the kids they know in school who are struggling. Pray for the schoolmate, their family, and opportunities for God to love them through you. Teaching your child to pray for struggling kids from an early age will help them not to envy that same kid's bad choices later in the teen years.

4. Whatever social or political sin of the day is being discussed, always emphasize to your child the positive side of God's view of the sin. For example, instead of calling all pro-choice adherents "baby killers," focus on how each one of us is fearfully and wonderfully made and how our heavenly Father knits us specifically and uniquely in our mother's womb. Brainstorm with your child how you can help a lost world see the beauty and necessity of protecting these tiniest of God's creation.

5. Make every day of your child's life have holy purpose. Begin praying with your children every morning. I know what you're thinking. You barely have enough time to stuff a Pop-Tart down your kid's gullet, much less spend time in prayer with them. I understand, but these five minutes are worth it. Help your child to pray the following things. In fact, teach your child to SHOUT these things every morning.

a. Share my faith with someone who doesn't know You today.

b. Help me to shine Your light in a dark place today.

c. Open my eyes to befriend someone who is alone today.

d. Use me to love someone who is hurting today.

e. Tell someone about the hope that is inside me today.

3

Institute Preparation–Based Parenting

Steve and Rhonda were two of the greatest Christian parents I knew. They attended my FamilyLife class at church every week and always contributed to the discussion with wisdom and insight. One evening, after class was over, they approached me with concerned faces and said they needed to talk. I zipped up my backpack and told them I was all ears. Steve began by saying they had great relationships with their kids, including an open dialogue with their two teenagers about a whole host of subjects. Rhonda continued, "Well, Jonathan [their sixteen-year-old] came home from lacrosse practice the other night and asked us which of the two creation stories in Genesis was true. He said a friend who played with him on the team pointed out that in one story man was created first and helped God name all the animals, and in the other story man was created last as God's crowning creation. He asked us which one was true and which one was false! Well, there's nothing false in the Bible, is there? I didn't even know there were two

> creation stories . . . Are there two creation stories? We were
> totally caught off guard and ended up mumbling something
> about how God works in mysterious ways, and we need to
> trust . . ." She looked sheepishly at Steve and said, "I really
> think we messed that up."

What earnest, sincere Christian parents! In the previous chapter, we discussed why it is critical for us to stop allowing fear to be the dominant influence in our parenting choices. But what should that dominant influence be? What should be the guiding principle behind how we raise our kids to be the godly adults Christ desires for them to be?

It's a concept we've steadily gotten away from: *preparation*. From the moment we look into our children's angelic eyes for the first time, our goal should be to prepare them. Prepare them to live a life independently dependent on God as their sole source and strength. Prepare them to rely on the presence of the Holy Spirit to sustain them regardless of their life circumstances. And finally, prepare them to exist outside the safe confines of our Christian homes and not to fear culture but engage it, making an impact for the gospel of Christ in their generation.

Presently, we spend the majority of our time as parents desperately trying to keep our children safely out of the battle with our increasingly secular culture. We're afraid the coarse language, sexual promiscuity, and rampant secular humanism that saturates their schools and peer groups will corrupt their souls and shred their spirits. We are so afraid of how the culture is going to negatively impact their faith that we do everything we can to keep them out of the fight. But aren't we all blessed and glad that no one kept a young David out of the fight with the Philistines, his opposing godless culture? Some people tried to keep him away, but he still confronted Goliath, and history was forever changed.

We reference young David again because we must understand that our kids have giants of their own to vanquish. How can we stand in the way of God using His children for His purposes? Instead of keeping them locked in our homes, let's spend the precious years we have with our kids preparing them to enter the cultural coliseum and win that fight!

Dr. Gary Habermas taught one of my doctoral seminars. If you have read *The Case for Christ* by Lee Strobel, you might recognize his name. Strobel interviewed Dr. Habermas for that book because he is the leading authority on the historicity of Christ's resurrection. For decades, he has debated atheistic academic dignitaries from all over the world who apply all their scholarly acumen to convince the academic panel or audience of those debates that the resurrection of Jesus did not factually, historically happen. He has debated several renowned atheists. For example, he debated the leading philosophical atheist in the world at that time, British philosopher Antony Flew.

In that class, he regaled us with stories from many of those debates about what his opponents would do and how he would counter with his own well-reasoned arguments. But one day during a break, I went up to Dr. Habermas and said, "You've been telling us of all the arguments and debating points that you used that were successful when you won your debates. But what tactics and arguments did they use against you, those times they won the debate?" I'll never forget the puzzled look on his face when he responded, "Well, as far as I know, I never lost."

I, for lack of a better word, was stunned. In all those debates, over all those years, against some of the greatest minds of the past century, Dr. Habermas never lost an academic debate about whether the resurrection of Jesus Christ historically happened? I couldn't believe it. Can you believe it? When Christians engage secular culture, even the upper echelon of academia, we don't just do okay; we metaphorically kick butt and take names! We do not have to fear the godless influence of this culture. This culture should fear us—and the impact our well-prepared children will have on it.

Our culture contains a paradigm taught in every secondary school and college, espoused on TV shows and movies, and reinforced in the mainstream media that says smart, educated, sophisticated, open-minded, and tolerant people do not believe in God, and the rural, uneducated, simplistic hate mongers cling to their guns and religion. This covert and overt message bombards our kids on an almost daily basis. It is critical that we begin to refute this misconception in the minds of our kids. Why? Because it is factually incorrect. Here are a few examples of extremely smart, successful people who also believe in Scripture and that Jesus is Lord:

- Francis S. Collins, MD, PhD, head of the Human Genome Project
- Neil Armstrong (1930–2012), first person to walk on the face of the moon
- Brant Cryder, president of Yves Saint Laurent North America
- Denzel Washington, Academy Award–winning actor

- heads of notable corporations, such as Hobby Lobby, Domino's Pizza, Chick-fil-A, and Interstate Batteries
- the vast majority of presidents of the United States
- oh, and a ton of Nobel Prize winners

This isn't a list of uneducated simpletons. We need to understand, and our kids need to understand, that many intelligent and successful people believe in God the Father and His Son Jesus Christ. This is true of the past as well—many bright and productive people throughout history have been Christ-followers. When we take a stand for faith in Christ, we are not taking a subordinate intellectual position. And we are certainly not alone in assuming that belief.

How Are We Supposed to Prepare Our Kids to Win the Culture War?

In his excellent book *Age of Opportunity,* Paul David Tripp encourages parents not to spend their energy on keeping their kids "out of the ring" when confronting culture but to vigorously train them to win the fight once they get in the ring. So the big question is—how do we do this? How are Christian parents supposed to prepare their children to be so equipped in their faith that the gates of their high school will not prevail against them (see Matt. 16:18)? Well, the church and the Christian home have done a fairly good job of teaching Bible facts. Most kids active in the church can tell you who Paul was or where Jesus was crucified. For the most part, our kids know *what* they believe. What they seem to lack is an understanding of *why* they believe it.

We begin the process of preparing our kids to confront culture by teaching them the *why*. We need to begin vigorously teaching our kids *apologetics*. Have you ever heard that word? It's a tad obscure, but chances are you've heard it tossed around by your pastor from time to time. It probably falls into the category of "church words" that we hear but don't necessarily understand. Words like *vicarious, sanctification, regeneration, justification*, or even *discipleship* are common in church services, yet many of us don't have any idea what they actually mean.

The word *apologetics* simply means a defense of the faith. First Peter 3:15 states, "But sanctify Christ as Lord in your hearts, *always being ready to make a defense* to everyone who asks you to give an account for the hope that is in you, yet with gentleness and reverence" (NASB, emphasis added). So Scripture is asking us to be prepared, to be ready to defend our faith. Why did Peter demand this? Because he knew in his day, as well as in ours, the Christian faith would need defending against a deceived and doubting world. Peter was exhorting us, as followers of Christ, to be ready to answer questions from those around us who may be skeptical about Christianity. That means being ready to answer questions like:

- Why is the Bible true but the Qur'an isn't?
- How can you prove God exists?
- Doesn't evolution prove there is no God?
- How can an intelligent person believe the Bible when it was written thousands of years ago?
- Isn't the Bible full of contradictions?
- How can a supposedly loving God send a good person to hell?

- Don't all faiths basically worship the same god, just in different ways?
- What makes Christianity right and all other religions wrong?
- If God is all-powerful and all-loving, why do evil and suffering exist in the world?
- How can someone say Jesus is the only way to God?

So, Mom and Dad, how do you think your teenager will do when a nonbeliever asks them one of these questions? Because if this type of questioning of their faith hasn't happened yet, it will very soon. And it is your job to make sure they are prepared to answer such inquiries—not by sending them to church to learn the magic words but by addressing these types of questions in the course of your daily encounters with them.

I remember facing similar challenges from my classmates like it was yesterday. I was a junior in high school, sitting in study hall, when the subject of having sex before marriage came up. Several of us were sitting around bantering this back and forth, when I simply proclaimed that sex before marriage was wrong because the Bible said that it was wrong. Period. End of discussion. Let's move on to the next topic. But a buddy of mine looked at me and said, "Well, I don't believe in the Bible, so what else ya got?" Problem was I actually didn't have anything else. "For the Bible tells me so" was the full extent of my arsenal. And that's when the realization hit me that I knew what I believed; I just didn't know why I believed it.

In that moment, in front of those other kids, my faith took its first shot to the gut, but that incident set me on a course of study to understand why I believed the Bible to be true. Over time, I learned that Christianity is all about faith, yes, but it's not a blind faith. It is an intelligent faith. A faith based on historically verifiable facts. I was determined not to be caught off guard ever again.

So you were asked how you thought your kids would do if asked those questions. A better question might be, how do you think *you* would do? You may have already had to deal with being stumped by a deep theological question. In fact, your own kids might have asked you some of those questions. If so, how did you handle it?

Of course, all parents are not expected to have a seminary degree and a black belt in theological debating. But when our kids are stumped by a question about their faith, it can be a tad unnerving when they come to us for help and all we can offer is a blank stare. In fact, they may begin to think these tough questions have no answers, causing the seeds of doubt, disenchantment, or disinterest to begin to grow.

This Is Not about Knowing All the Answers, so Take a Deep Breath

I became a Christian when I was fifteen years old, and I was completely fascinated by my newfound faith. I attended First Baptist Church in Cisco, Texas, and every Sunday night after services, my pastor, Brother Buddy Sipe, would leave the sanctuary, grab two Pepsis out of the machine, and go to his office and wait for me to arrive. Within minutes, here I'd come, prepared to ask him all the questions about Christianity that I had thought of throughout the preceding week. Then I would begin to pepper him with such profound theological queries as, "Where did Cain get his wife?" and "Are the pygmies that have never heard the name Jesus going to go to hell?" and "Can God make a rock so big that He Himself can't lift it?"

To his credit, he never laughed or downplayed my curiosity. Rather, he would take all the time in the world to search the Bible and patiently try to answer my questions. There were times, however, that he simply didn't know the answer. And he would actually say that he didn't know. But he would also say, "Listen, Jimmy, I'll do some research about that one and get back with you next week." And he always would. Not only would he try to address the issue, but he also would show me where he went to find the answers. He introduced me to a Bible dictionary, Bible commentaries, and a concordance. I never knew such tools existed—resources, prior to Google, designed to help a believer study and understand God's Word. My pastor taught me an invaluable lesson all those Sunday evenings: just because I didn't know the answer to a God question didn't mean an answer didn't exist. It just meant I hadn't yet found the place that contained that answer.

You know, people ask very few original questions in regard to Christianity. Did Judas fall from a tree or jump off a cliff? Asked and answered. Did Adam and Eve really exist or did they simply represent the first men and women God created? Again, asked countless times and answered countless times. Throughout the past two thousand years, these types of questions have been asked and answered on innumerable occasions. What's more, they've been answered to the intellectual satisfaction of some of the brightest people in the history of humankind. So, as a parent, just because you may not know the answer to a particular question doesn't mean that question has not been addressed in an intellectually satisfactory way for a long, long time. You just have to know where to go to get that answer.

So Where Do You Go to Get That Answer?

We always need to keep in mind that we can't lead our children to a deeper level of discipleship than we have achieved ourselves. It is imperative that we, as parents, commit ourselves to study for the purpose of learning information that will help us, as Peter would say, defend the hope that is within us (see 1 Pet. 3:15). The good news is that there is no need to invent the theological wheel all over again. Many books deal with all the issues and topics we have been discussing. Step number one in becoming prepared is to get your hands on these books. Read what you can, and keep the rest on your bookshelf to use as reference materials when and if you may need them. Below is a small sampling of valuable books that will help you and your kids defend the faith:

- *The Case for Christ* by Lee Strobel
    How do we know the Bible is true to begin with? How can we trust that Jesus really existed and did and said all those things? This is an amazingly easy-to-understand guide to basic apologetics.
- *The Case for Faith* by Lee Strobel
    This book, which is easy to read and understand, addresses the eight big questions that have plagued Christianity since the beginning. For example, how can evil and suffering exist if God is all-powerful and all-loving? How come the God of the Old Testament seems to be

much harsher and more vengeful than the God of the New Testament?

- *The Big Book of Christian Apologetics: An A to Z Guide* by Norman Geisler
The title says it all. This book addresses all aspects of defending the Christian faith.
- *The Questions Christians Hope No One Will Ask (with Answers)* by Mark Mittelberg and Lee Strobel
Questions like: Why are Christians against same-sex marriage? How could a loving God send people to hell? And many more.
- *Keeping Your Kids on God's Side* by Natasha Crain
This is a wonderful book to introduce the idea of answering questions about Christianity to younger children.
- *Mere Christianity* by C. S. Lewis
This is a classic.
- *The Apologetics Study Bible* by Holman Bible Publishers
More than a hundred key questions and articles are placed throughout this Bible that address important aspects of apologetics.
- *Prove It: Defend the Christian Faith* by Stephen Cutchins
This helpful guide hits home with the Millennial generation.
- *How Now Shall We Live?* by Charles Colson
This excellent book gives the most reasoned argument for holding to a Christian worldview you will ever read. Great stuff!
- *Evidence That Demands a Verdict* by Josh McDowell
As a college student, McDowell had deep doubts about Christianity and set out to prove it was a

fraudulent faith. His life was forever changed by the excessive evidence he discovered proving that what the Bible says is true and real. This compelling book shares that evidence in regard to numerous common objections to Christianity.

See? You don't have to have a seminary degree. You just have to do a little book shopping. Make sure you have several of these books, familiarize yourself with them, and walk through the material with your kids. Two thousand years ago, Peter said to "be ready" to give a defense of the hope that is within us. That command has never changed.

We Will Never Argue Anyone into Heaven

Let's look at 1 Peter 3:15 again. Peter implores, "But sanctify Christ as Lord in your hearts, always being ready to make a defense to everyone who asks you to give an account for the hope that is in you, *yet with gentleness and reverence*" (NASB, emphasis added). So not only are we, as believers, to be ready to give an account of our hope in Christ, but we are also to make that defense with gentleness and reverence. *The Message* paraphrases it like this: "Be ready to speak up and tell anyone who asks why you're living the way you are, *and always with the utmost courtesy*" (emphasis added). As you can see, we are to do it "with the utmost courtesy" as well.

Here's an important rule to remember: you will never argue anyone into heaven. I'm sure it's probably happened, but I've never seen it. Perhaps you've heard of this scenario: a Christian and a non-Christian are arguing about an aspect of the faith when the non-Christian stops, lowers his head, and says, "You're right. You've always been right, and I've always been wrong. In fact, my entire secular worldview has now been destroyed. Tell me, what must I do to be saved?" There's as much chance of that happening as a snowball's chance in Hades.

Defending our faith is not about winning an argument. Arguments rarely serve a useful purpose. They tend to get personal and produce lots of tension, and the problem at hand is rarely solved. This is why cable news shows in which everyone is yelling at one another can sometimes be hard to watch. Have you ever noticed that no one switches their opinion, so the argument is never won? Instead, defending our faith is about answering questions honestly and compassionately and to the best of our ability. That's all. Forget about changing a person's mind. Our job, and our children's job, is to demonstrate that there is a lucid, reasoned answer to any question posed about the Christian faith.

You can do this, Mom and Dad. You can prepare your child to engage this culture in a healthy manner. You can prepare your child to defend their faith. You can move them beyond simple Bible knowledge to a secure understanding that intellectually undergirds their faith. Here are five practical changes you can make today to facilitate this goal.

Five Practical Changes You Can Make Today

1. Jesus said in John 10:27 that His sheep would recognize His voice. Since fear is the opposite of faith, we must understand that He will never use fear to motivate us. So begin to recognize that the voice telling you to be afraid and to hold back your child is *not* the voice of

your Shepherd. Acknowledge fear as the voice of the Deceiver—and reject it.

2. Get several of the books mentioned in this chapter and read them. As difficult as it may be, force yourself to do the right thing. Read and discuss them with your child—especially the books that deal with the big questions that have plagued Christianity from the beginning. Hash out these topics with your child now so that when questions come up with their friends, they will not be caught off guard.

3. Be constantly at work building your apologetics library. These can be actual bound copies or digital versions, but either way, create a resource library that can help you and your child defend the faith with ease and convenience.

4. Search current events, news programs, and social media for issues that confront a biblical Christian worldview. Discuss with your child the issue, the challenges, and the biblical responses. Make this a normal aspect of your interaction with your child.

5. Always emphasize to your child that this training is not about winning an argument. Love, not a well-researched argument, reaches the lost. Our first and foremost calling from God is to love—responding well in a debate is secondary.

4

Taking Charge of Our Children's Spiritual Growth

Lucy and her husband had come to see me about their seventeen-year-old and very oppositional and defiant son, Chad. He not only was verbally defiant but also was doing drugs and having sex and currently on probation for shoplifting. Lucy sat on my couch and was clearly extremely upset. While she was fired up about her son's behavior, she was equally angry with their church, which she and her family had attended since Chad was a small child. She said, "I don't get it. We have taken him to that church since he was a little baby. He attended every VBS, Bible club, and Sunday school class they had to offer. We even made him go when he got into high school, even though he said he hated it. We spent so much money on camps and retreats and T-shirts! And for what? So he'd end up like this? What were they doing with him all that time? Didn't they teach him anything?" Then, realizing just how inappropriate

> her rant must have sounded, she sheepishly added, "Well, maybe we weren't the best parents when it comes to spiritual things, but come on, surely something should have stuck!"

Lucy is the perfect, if not overexaggerated, example of why parents should not outsource their children's spiritual growth. We, as Christian parents, must take full spiritual responsibility for our kids. We must take responsibility for their training and discipleship. Not the church, not the pastor, not even the youth minister. The spiritual buck stops with us.

This topic reminds me of a young man by the name of Jack. He was sixteen years old and had recently lost his mother to cancer and was suffering through a fairly intense battle with depression when I began counseling him. But he was not only depressed; he was also downright angry. Was he angry at the cruelty of life or at God for allowing his mother to endure such suffering? No, he was also spitting mad at his father, who seemed to be superspiritualizing their family's tragedy. The boy yearned to talk honestly with his dad about his grief, or just turn to him for comfort and assurance, but his father always responded with a stream of pious platitudes and Bible verses. Jack saw his dad as living in a state of spiritual denial, hiding behind Christian "bumper sticker" phrases meant to communicate hope but that only left Jack feeling cold and empty. When he reached out for his dad at the time of his greatest need and pain, all he received was a doctrinal lesson on how God would cause everything to work together for their good. True as that may be, it wasn't what this hurting young man needed from his dad in this season.

Jack had been quietly examining his belief in Christ for some time, and his mother's illness and ultimate death had left his faith dangerously weakened. The robotic spiritual response of his father in the midst of this life-altering family catastrophe put the wrecking ball to Jack's crumbling walls of belief. He bitterly told his dad, "If *this* is your faith, if *this* is all your religion is, then you can have it. I always thought this Christianity thing wasn't real . . . and now I *know* it's not."

Jack's view of Christianity is not unique. Many young people raised in Christian homes have a hard time "believing." Studies among preteens conducted by the Barna Group have revealed that only slightly more than half of eight- to twelve-year-olds believe in the God described in the Bible; less than half say their religious faith is very important to them today; just four out of ten claim the main purpose of life is to love God with all their heart and soul, mind and strength; and just one-third contend that the Bible is accurate in all that it teaches. One of the centerpieces of the Christian faith—the resurrection of Jesus—is believed by only one-third of them. About one-quarter believe Satan is real, and even fewer (19 percent) say they have a responsibility to share their faith with other people. Meanwhile, a majority of these youngsters maintain that Jesus Christ sinned while He lived on earth and that the Holy Spirit is just a symbol, not a living entity. The proportion of high school and college students who describe themselves as atheist, agnostic, or "none" has more than tripled in the past decade alone![1]

Poll after poll clearly shows that Americans, particularly young Americans, are fleeing the local church in shocking numbers. More and more people in this country report that they have stopped attending church and have given up practicing their faith in any meaningful way.[2] Among teenagers, about six out of ten will drop out of organized religious activity—yep, the local church—as soon as they leave home for college or other independent pursuits. One recent study showed that more than 60 percent of evangelical young adults *who reported being active in church during grade school and high school* were no longer attending church by the time they reached their mid- to upper twenties.[3]

Denominationalism isn't the answer either. Attendance is down in virtually every mainline denomination, baptisms are down, and memberships are down, with no real recovery in sight. Most of the churches associated with evangelical denominations are struggling to connect with young people as well. No matter what angle you approach it from, the results are similar—young believers are leaving the church. Ever since Jesus ascended into heaven, God has charged every generation with the task of reaching the society in which they live with the life-changing gospel of Christ. Our task as believers has always been to regenerate ourselves. Our primary calling as parents is to pass the love of Christ along to our children and our children's children. This myopic mandate is made quite clear throughout Scripture. Passing on the heart of our faith to the hearts of our children is now, and has always been, our premiere priority before God.

Since young believers are leaving the Christian faith in droves, our generation of twenty-first-century parents is apparently failing at this task. Those of us living in America today who call ourselves Christians should find our hearts gripped by the words of Hebrews 12:1: "Therefore, since we are surrounded by such a great cloud of witnesses, let us throw off everything that hinders and the sin that so easily entangles. And let us run with perseverance the race marked out for us."

So who is in this "great cloud of witnesses"? Well, the author of Hebrews gives a brief description a few verses earlier, when he identifies the many individuals down through history

who through faith conquered kingdoms, administered justice, and gained what was promised; who shut the mouths of lions, quenched the fury of the flames, and escaped the edge of the sword. . . . Some faced jeers and flogging, and even chains and imprisonment. They were put to death by stoning; they were sawed in two; they were killed by the sword. They went about in sheepskins and goatskins, destitute, persecuted and mistreated—the world was not worthy of them. (11:33–34, 36–38)

So what happened when it came time for *our* generation to run the race marked out for *us*? In front of this distinguished crowd of heaven-bound believers who suffered so much to pass their faith on to us, we dropped the baton.

Many people have looked at the current plight of Christianity in our country and have blamed the church. People have stopped coming to church, they say, because the music is old, the sermons are boring, and churches are no longer relevant. Others argue that the church is suffering because we live in an increasingly secular nation, and we've allowed its godless influence to erode our distinctives as followers of Christ.

I would have to agree that the church can certainly do things better, but I feel strongly that the current exodus from Christian faith in America should not be laid at the foot of the church alone. I would echo the words of an elderly man whose name I never knew but whose wisdom is well worth sharing.

I heard his words several years ago while participating in a task force appointed by the local school district to choose and implement the sex education curriculum for the secondary schools of that city. In one of the town hall meetings organized to discuss the issue, several citizens exercised their first amendment rights by excoriating the school board for every evil under the sun. And all these evils, in their opinion, could be traced back to the day America took prayer out of the public schools. They seemed convinced that if we just had prayer in the schools, there would be no need for sex education at all!

The critics continued their tirade for some time until an elderly man stood in the back of the auditorium and made this simple yet sobering statement: "Our problem is not that we don't have prayer in the public schools anymore. Our problem is that we don't have prayer in our homes anymore." That pretty much shut everybody up.

I believe the current downturn of Christianity in America is not a symptom of churches in crisis as much as it is a sign that our families are in spiritual crisis. Churches, for the most part, are made up of families. Christian families, therefore, are at the heart of this struggle.

A Parent's One Job

Several years ago, my son, Josh (whom I have the privilege of working with every day as one of my fellow counselors at our office), and I took an advanced scuba diving course out at Lake Travis, west of Austin.

One of the skills we had to master in this course was underwater navigation. Two divers paired together to navigate by compass from one underwater location to another. One partner's job was to work out all the calculations and count the fin strokes in order to find the correct destination; the other partner's sole job was to keep both divers at a depth of exactly thirty feet. I was the first to navigate, while Josh watched our depth. No one really had to point out that I was not very good at this particular diving skill. We ended up emerging from the water on the shores of a campground quite a distance from our specified destination. I was substantially embarrassed by this, and the small children swimming at the camp were terrified by the scary man making all the bubbles.

Then it was Josh's turn to do all the navigating, while my only responsibility was to keep us at a depth of thirty feet. As we began our nautical journey, I thought he was doing very well—much better than I had done, as a matter of fact. But about five minutes into the exercise, he abruptly stopped and looked at me with obvious exasperation. I shrugged my shoulders, the universal signal for "what's up?" He proceeded to grab me by the front of my gear and shoved me up about six inches . . . and my head popped out of the water. Needless to say, I had not done my job of keeping us at a depth of thirty feet. Ripping his mask off, he glared at me. "You had one job, Dad. Just one! I wasn't asking you to multitask or anything. You had only one job . . . and you blew it."

He was absolutely right. I did have only one job that day, and I did completely blow it. Similarly, I believe Christian parents today have one *primary* responsibility: to raise their children to love Christ and live a life that brings Him glory. Now, don't roll your eyes at me. Parents have a multitude of roles to fulfill and tasks to complete, but when it all gets boiled down to their most important duty as a believing parent, they still have that one *primary* job. And like me in the scuba class, many seem to be somewhat off course.

In what way are we falling short of our number one job? Let's be clear, we all love God. We all love our kids, go to church, and try to live the right way. So why in the world would I lay the apparent failure of all Christendom at the feet of beleaguered parents? Well, I certainly don't see the issue as a lack of effort. Today's parents are working themselves into early graves. They work longer hours, with fewer vacation days, than their European counterparts. They labor at second jobs and take extra shifts just to help make ends meet, and the last thing they need is to be told they have to do something else.

No, the issue is not lack of effort; it's failure of priority.

Let me explain. *Merriam-Webster's Dictionary* tells us that the word *stewardship* means "the careful and responsible management of something entrusted to one's care." So to be a good *steward* means to take good care of something that doesn't belong to you but that is on loan and is in your charge. Like me, you probably have heard in countless sermons that the biblical concept of stewardship refers to a believer's time, talents, and treasure. We understand that God has given us a finite amount of time on this earth, and we need to be good stewards of that time. God has given each of us unique talents and abilities, and we must be good stewards of those gifts and use them for His glory. And all the treasure we have comes from God, and we are mandated to be good stewards of those monies and materials.

For our purposes, let's consider the concept of stewardship as it pertains to our children. These little ones are the greatest gifts we will ever have to take care of. Each believer blessed with children has the capacity to be an instrument in God's hands to mold and shape them into His image to be used for His purposes. Paul emphasized the idea of stewardship when he implored his young protégé, Timothy, to "guard what has been entrusted to your care" (1 Tim. 6:20). And that, in my opinion, is the bottom line. Too many Christian parents are simply not doing a very good job of guarding *the most important thing* entrusted to their care, namely, their children and their children's relationship with Christ. Their priorities often lie elsewhere. Other things seem to be more important than the spiritual growth and welfare of their kids. Oh, don't get me wrong, their children's faith in Christ is important; it's just that it ranks about number five or six on their list.

Of course, most of us are so busy from day to day that we don't have much opportunity to evaluate where we're investing our lives, which naturally leads me to duck hunting. Have you ever been duck hunting? If so, you know how it works: you find a pond, throw out a bunch of decoys, and blow a duck call to attract the incoming ducks. As your quarry flies in, they see something that looks like a duck, they hear something that quacks like a duck, but, of course, decoys are not ducks. They are imposters.

Many of the parents I interact with in my practice seem focused on "decoy" priorities. The urgent matters that consume their time and energy look important, sound important, and, in fact, everyone else in society deems them to be important, but, ultimately, they are not. They are, in fact, imposters. And many of these fake priorities are not bad things. Careers, homes, cars, recreational activities, personal success, and our children's achievements—these pursuits are not bad in and of themselves. But when they replace the supremacy of God's will in the life of your family, they morph into something destructive.

A good job is a great thing, a blessing from God. But when your family suffers from a parent's obsessive pursuit of career goals, then it becomes an imposter. Having close friendships is a wonderful thing. In fact, it's important for all parents to maintain these close bonds for camaraderie and account-ability. But when hanging with your friends stands between you and God's purposes for your family, then bonding be-comes a negative thing. Wanting your children to succeed is good, and setting high standards can lead them in positive directions. But when their success is how you measure your own success, this desire stops being encouraging and starts being caustic and self-centered, and it eats away at a child's sense of worth.

So many parents are so busy chasing decoy priorities that the really important duties, as assigned by our heav-enly Father, get shoved to the end of the list. Remember the old saying "If Satan can't make you bad, he'll make you busy"? I've found that most old sayings got to be old sayings because they tend to be true. Most of the parents I work with are running at breakneck speed, without one second to spare, in a desperate attempt to do everything, be everything, and keep up with everything the Joneses are accumulating next door. And what do we do when we are faced with too many competing priorities? Well, like the good delegators we are, we opt to outsource some of those priorities. Most important, we often delegate the spiritual development of our own children to others.

Outsourcing Our Kids' Faith

If you remember, Lucy and her husband were quite busy taking their son to church events. And that's all great. But I'm pretty sure there's more to shepherding our children's souls than guiding them through the doors of a local church on a regular basis.

I believe that one of the most detrimental aspects of church growth over the centuries began when early believers were first introduced to the professional clergy. There wasn't always a paid preacher down at the church, you know. In fact, Frank Viola and George Barna, in their book *Pagan Christianity?*, assert that "up until the second century the church had no official leadership. That it had leaders is without dispute. But leadership was unofficial in the sense that there were no religious 'offices' or sociological slots to fill."[4]

During the first century, it was all hands on deck. Everyone worked together to spread the gospel and minister to the demands of those within the church and those in need outside the church. But with the advent of professional clergy, the rank-and-file membership soon began to view these "called" men as the professionals and began to rely more and more on them to do the actual work of the ministry.

I was a youth minister for almost twenty years before entering the counseling field, and it never ceased to amaze me how many parents would call for one of the pastors at the church to come speak with their child who was asking questions about becoming a Christian. Now, most of these parents had been attending church services, classes, and other events their whole lives. Over the years, they were regularly exposed to the teachings of the Bible as they sat through an incalculable number of sermons, conferences, and studies. Yet when this magical, mystical, miraculous moment occurred in the life of their child, when the blessed opportunity actually came to talk to their son or daughter about faith and to pray with their child to receive Christ as their Savior, they called the preacher to come do it.

Sadly, many of us Christian parents have developed the attitude that our only responsibility before God on behalf of our kids is to be their spiritual taxi drivers. We've concluded that our job is simply to drop them off at camp, get them to Sunday school, and make sure they attend the youth retreat, while the real responsibility of their salvation and spiritual growth has been outsourced to the children's minister, youth minister, or pastor. Parents have to reassume this all-important duty. We must once again take spiritual responsibility for our children. We must realize that our number one job, *without a close second*, is to guide and nurture our children's faith in Christ, to accept those precious eternal souls as our primary responsibility—and no one else's.

Why Our Kids Are Leaving Their Faith

Let's say we were to round up a bunch of non-Christian teenagers and ask them why they don't believe in the Christian faith. Very few would list satanic rock musicians, misogynistic rap artists, the influence of fervent atheists, or the theory of evolution taught in their science classes. Instead, the number one answer we would hear is that the church is full of hypocrites. This is not much of a surprise. Very few people actively reject Christ; they are rejecting Christians. They are rejecting you and me. That believers are not living a genuine, authentic, and relevant faith—the fact that few Christians act like Christians—is what most would consider the number one reason young people say they are rejecting the Christian faith in the twenty-first century. They seem to be echoing the words of Mahatma Gandhi, who was famously quoted as saying, "I like your Christ, I do not like your Christians. Your Christians are so unlike your Christ."[5] Brennan Manning put it this way: "The greatest single cause of atheism in the world today is Christians: who acknowledge Jesus with their lips, walk out the door, and deny Him by their lifestyle. That is what an unbelieving world simply finds unbelievable"[6] Ouch! But isn't this exactly what our kids are telling us?

And for kids who have grown up active in church, in believing homes, with believing parents, which "Christians" don't they like? What are the most obvious Christian examples in their lives that they are rejecting as hypocritical? That's right, Mom and Dad. They are talking about us—parents who claim faith in Christ, then live a life that essentially denies any authentic relationship with Him.

The exodus of young adults from the Christian faith in America should serve as a wake-up call for us to get our spiritual acts together before our lukewarm faith has an even more detrimental effect on our children's generation. We have to begin living what we say we believe if we are to have any hope of communicating to our kids that our faith is real, the Bible is true, and Jesus is the Way, the Truth, and the Life. Whether or not we are comfortable with it, living a life of authentic example is our calling, and regaining influence with this present generation is our mandate.

It's been said that when the game is on the line, when the last seconds are ticking off the clock, and when the outcome hinges on the very last play, the greatest pros of all time always want the ball in their hands. Jerry Rice, Michael Jordan, Kobe Bryant, and Larry Bird would all tell you, "When it's crunch time, give me the ball." In their playing days, they *wanted* the responsibility of winning the game to rest solely with them. Well, it's crunch time. The game is winding down to the last seconds, and whether or not you like it, want it, or think you're up to it, the souls of your children rest on your shoulders. The outcome of the game is in your hands. But the most sobering thought? *This is not a game.*

Five Practical Changes You Can Make Today

1. Pray that God will give you the strength and courage to rearrange some of your priorities to make your child's spiritual growth your top priority. Also pray for wisdom and discernment in this area to know what to say, what to do, and how to do it.

2. Do not simply take your child to church; exemplify a vibrant walk with Christ for them. Incorporate your relationship with Christ into everything that occurs in your family's life and weave Christ-centered priorities into the nooks and crannies of everyday living. They must see that God lives outside the walls of the church building and is active and present in every moment of your family's existence.

3. Praying with your child must incorporate more than "Now I lay me down to sleep" or "Bless this food to the nourishment of our bodies." Your child must see that you cling to prayer. Help them understand that prayer is the foundation of all major life decisions as well as the countless concerns of your everyday life.

4. Initiate spiritual discussions on a regular basis so they become normal, not uncomfortable. Be aware of those teachable moments that God brings into your life and take advantage of them.

5. What is your child studying in their church Bible study and youth group each week? Do you know? Well, find out, and discuss these issues at home, around the dinner table, or before going to bed. What is your child's opinion about these things? Don't minimize their views or try to impress them with your superior knowledge. Encourage them, praise them, let them express their true feelings and beliefs, but never fail to guide them to the truth of Scripture.

5

Our Children Are Called
to Stand Out

Helen, mom of thirteen-year-old Abby, was telling me recently how disappointed she was in the way her daughter was dressing. She often cringed when Abby would leave the house because she felt that her clothing was inappropriate for her age and her Christian faith. Apparently, her daughter was wearing very short shorts and revealing tops on a regular basis. In frustration, Helen stated, "I'm embarrassed to let her out at school! She looks like an absolute @#$%!" I asked Helen where her daughter got the clothes to start with, and she confirmed that she had, in fact, purchased them for Abby. When I challenged her on this obvious lack of consistency, she admitted, "Well, I don't like buying her those kinds of clothes, but I don't want her to stand out like a sore thumb! Every other girl in her class wears the same thing! I want her to fit in with all her friends."

Up to this point, we've been discussing parents who go overboard protecting and segregating their children from the evil influences of secular culture, but what about those parents who don't separate their kids from culture at all? They, in fact, embrace culture and, in some ways, allow their children to be overwhelmed by and absorbed into the secular worldview of their peers. When it comes to parenting differently and, therefore, producing kids who are different, many parents freeze up at the thought. We so desperately want our kids to be happy, and to fit in with all the other kids in school, that we often lower our moral and behavioral standards. Our kids don't want to stand out, and we don't want them to either, so we involve them in all the same activities and purchase them the same clothes and gadgets that the secular culture says they should have. But if we stop and consider this for a moment, we might realize that secular culture is making the parenting decisions in our families and not us. It is this current parenting practice that we would now like to address.

Now, before you begin pointing out the apparent inconsistency between this chapter and a couple of previous chapters, which call for encouraging our kids to engage culture, not retreat from it, let me explain. There is a difference between engaging culture with a well-prepared, Christ-centered purpose and simply surrendering to a godless culture and embracing all that comes with it. I can hear some of you saying, "Well, what about Jesus? He hung out with sinners all the time!" True, He did. But His purpose in being with those people was to transform their lives, not trade vodka shots with them. There is a difference.

86

Testing Produces Perseverance

Have you ever heard a parent say that all they want is for their child to be happy? Sure you have. This seems to have become the dominant desire of so many parents today. Part of the reason may be that happiness has become the foundation of the worldview of most Americans, regardless of age. I've heard parents say happiness is a constitutional right—life, liberty, and the pursuit of happiness. (They don't get too hung up on the presence of that pesky phrase "the pursuit of" that always seems to emerge in front of their "right.") It's not surprising that if most parents are devoted to achieving happiness, then they want their children to be happy as well.

Parents these days seem dedicated to meeting every need and want their children have. We don't want our children to experience any negative outcome, so we stay up all night making the papier-mâché volcano, actually doing their homework for them, and stalk their social media accounts to make sure they are not being mistreated by any of their peers. We want them to have everything, do everything, and wear everything that will make them fit safely and snuggly into their secular peer groups. We don't want our little darlings to fret about a thing, endure anything remotely unpleasant, or stand out in any way. But is this the way our heavenly Father parents us? Remember, if our overarching parental principle is being to our children as God is to us, is this how God is to us? Does He make sure we don't fret about a thing, experience anything remotely unpleasant, or stand out in a secular culture?

In fact, I see many parents get angry because God doesn't parent the way they do. When He does allow difficulties into our lives and doesn't swoop in to miraculously rescue us from predicaments of our own making, we question His love for us. We question whether He really is as all-powerful as He says He is. Isn't it odd that we question God because He doesn't adopt our parenting style, instead of questioning ourselves because we haven't adopted His?

Nowhere in Scripture does God promise us happiness or a carefree life. In fact, He promises quite the opposite. Second Timothy 3:12 tells us, "In fact, everyone who wants to live a godly life in Christ Jesus will be persecuted." Standing out from the crowd, experiencing rejection from a secular culture, and suffering persecution at the hands of nonbelievers is a promise to every one of us who is called by His name. And this is not because God is maniacal and loves watching His children agonize. He allows this persecution into our lives because He knows it is ultimately good for us and our relationship with him. It's sort of God's version of "no pain, no gain." James 1:2–4 puts it this way: "Consider it pure joy, my brothers and sisters, whenever you face trials of many kinds, because you know that the testing of your faith produces perseverance. Let perseverance finish its work so that you may be mature and complete, not lacking anything."

So it seems that the Word of God is fairly clear that we should not be trying to keep our children away from the persecution of secular culture. We should welcome it as a necessary part of our kids' discipleship process. Our kids (and us) are never closer to the heart of Christ than when we experience hardship in His name. So we are not supposed to bend over backward to make sure our kids fit in with those around them but, rather, "rejoice inasmuch as you participate in the sufferings of Christ, so that you may be overjoyed when his glory is revealed" (1 Pet. 4:13).

Come On, Mom, Everybody Is Going!

"But so-and-so will be there. I have to go! Everyone is going!" What parent has not found themselves on the receiving end of this challenge? Your child wants to have something, do something, or go somewhere, and you, the parent, are caught between doing what you feel is in the best interest of your child and going against your better judgment simply so your child can fit in with their friends. Do we follow what we believe is the most Christ-honoring choice for our children or allow them to participate in dubious activities with everyone else?

> Liz told me she was perplexed by what was going on with her daughter, Emily, and Emily's high school drill team. When I pressed her further, she said, "I went to pick her and her best friend up from practice the other day and watched them for a few minutes until they were done. Well, I was shocked by the song they were dancing to. It was lewd, sexually suggestive, and even though they bleeped out the profanity, the intended foul language was blatantly obvious. So when my daughter and her friend got in the car, I asked her about the song. They both laughed as though I were kidding. When I told them I wasn't kidding and that I thought the song was completely inappropriate for a high school dance team, my daughter got upset and told me not to make a big deal out of it or complain to the director or make any waves. Then she told me how embarrassed she was to be with me! How she was embarrassed with me!" So I asked Liz what she eventually did about the situation, and she said, "Well, nothing. Emily is just a sophomore and didn't want the older girls making fun of her because of me. But that Friday night at the football game they danced to that song, and all the

> *other kids and parents were just clapping and singing along.*
> *Oh, and my parents were there too. Thank the Lord their*
> *hearing is awful!"*

Liz is just like most of the Christian parents in America: struggling to walk what seems like a fine line between sensitivity to her child's needs and obedience to God's Word. (For what it's worth, the line may not be as "fine" as we think.) A recent survey by the American Culture & Faith Institute among conservative Christian parents found that only one-third of them claim to consistently make choices that emphasize their child's character and witness rather than those more likely to make the child comfortable.[1]

Of course, "going along to get along" is nothing new. It's been around for at least a couple thousand years. Paul offers a great example of this in Galatians. Since Paul was charged by God to take the gospel to the Gentiles, he was hounded by the Judaizers, former Jews who insisted a person had to be a good Jew first, then they could be a Christian. And being a good Jew meant following all the rites, rituals, and festivals of the Jewish faith as a pathway to Christ. The believers in Galatia whom Paul was writing to were being instructed to continue all those rites and rituals to be good Christians. And Paul, of course, was telling these new believers that faith was all they needed and not to worry about works of righteousness. In Galatians 6:12, he, in fact, addresses the motivations of these Judaizers and their persistence about new Gentile converts being circumcised when he writes, "Those who want to impress people by means of the flesh are trying to compel you to be circumcised. The only reason they do this is to avoid being persecuted for the cross of Christ." See? They were doing something wrong just to avoid being persecuted by those they feared. Sound familiar? Allowing our kids to be in a non–Christ-honoring place, doing non–Christ-honoring things simply to avoid the rejection of their secular peers is to suck all the power out of the cross of Christ.

To simply avoid being laughed at, talked about, left out, not invited, or not "friended" on social media is not a defensible reason to deny our faith with our actions. It is essential that we teach our kids to love God more than they fear the rejection of their peer group. What was it that Paul said in Romans? Oh yeah: "What, then, shall we say in response to these things? If God is for us, who can be against us?" (8:31). Christians throughout history have lost everything for the gospel. A relationship with Christ has cost believers their lives and the lives of their families, and we're having a hard time keeping our kids from attending certain events that are inconsistent with their faith.

And let's make no mistake, it's not just Christians a long time ago who were persecuted for their faith. Followers of Christ today in the Sudan, Syria, and Iraq face death every day because of their faith. This is true in parts of Asia as well. In his excellent book *Radical: Taking Back Your Faith from the American Dream*, David Platt recounts meeting two teenagers in an underground church in an undisclosed part of Asia. Let me repeat—*two teenagers*! Their names were Shan and Ling, and they had been sent to undergo intense training in preparation for taking the gospel to parts of Asia where there were not even any underground churches. Platt recounts, "Ling said to me, 'I have told my family that I will likely never come back home. I am going to hard places to make the gospel known, and it is possible that I will lose my life in the process.' Shan added, 'But our families understand. Our moms and dads have been in prison for their faith, and they have taught us that Jesus is worthy of all our devotion.'"[2]

Okay, Mom and Dad, have we taught our children that Jesus is worthy of *all* our devotion? Or have we taught them that Jesus is worthy of our devotion only up until that devotion becomes slightly awkward, embarrassing, or uncomfortable? If you answer the latter, then have we taught them that it's okay to just silently go along with the secular crowd so that we don't rock the boat and can continue to fit in? There is a now-famous quote from a Christian in China that says, "You Christians in America are praying that we Christians in China will survive our persecution. But we Christians in China are praying for you Christians in America that you will survive your prosperity." And when you look at the vitality of the churches in China compared to those in America, the truth is pretty evident. They have survived their persecution, and we haven't survived our prosperity.

I'm the father of three and the grandfather of five, so I know how difficult it is to allow your child to experience hardship. But may we never forget that the hardship our kids here in America are being asked to endure for their faith is laughable compared to the hardships and persecution faced by so many Christian kids around the world.

One Quick Note about "Everybody Is Doing It!"

During one memorable week, I counseled two high school students who both loved the new school they were attending. The first was a big, strapping football player, and he said, "Dude, check it out, everybody smokes weed and parties. No lie, I mean, like *everybody*! It's, like, totally awesome. Like, I love this place." The next day I saw a young woman, and she said that she loved the same new school because "it is like a Christian school! Everybody goes to Bible studies and everybody has accountability partners. No, like, *everybody*! Like, I love this place."

Reality check: everybody is not doing it. At any given school, your child is going to know and keep up with about twenty kids. Now, if they are attending a large urban high school, that would be twenty kids out of about three thousand. So when they tell you, "Come on, Dad, *everybody* smokes weed!" What they are really saying is, "Come on, Dad, all the friends I know and hang out with smoke weed!" So in essence, when your child uses the "everybody is doing it" rationale for bad behavior, all they are really doing is indicting the kids they choose to associate with. So instead of motivating you to allow them to participate in the activity, it should motivate you to address the unfortunate peer group they have become a part of.

In the World but Not of the World

Several years ago, I was speaking to a large congregation in South America. I, of course, couldn't speak the native language, so I was speaking through an interpreter. During my talk, I made the statement, "When I became a Christian, I drank as much as I wanted to, did as many drugs as I wanted to, and slept with as many women as I wanted to. The difference was that I didn't want to. After I became a Christian, my 'want tos' changed." When the meeting was over, I was feeling quite good about how things had gone, when

an English-speaking missionary came up to me with a concerned look on his face. "That interpreter did not say what
you thought he would say!" he said. "He interpreted what you
were saying as, 'When I became a Christian, I drank much alcohol, I took many drugs, and I slept with many women!'" No
wonder so many people came forward during the invitation!

An embarrassing story to be sure, but what I was trying to
say is still true. Once a person commits their life to Christ,
they are different. Their "want tos" change. My favorite verse
in the entire Bible puts it this way: "Therefore, if anyone is
in Christ, the new creation has come: The old has gone, the
new is here!" (2 Cor. 5:17). So if all things have become new
in a believer's life, what is so appealing to our kids about
participating in an activity that completely contradicts what
they say they believe?

That's also a good question for us, as parents, to consider. Do our kids see us come home after we have had too
much to drink at the office get-togethers? Do they notice us
watching movies that are clearly in contradiction to our pro-
fessed beliefs? Do they hear our language get coarser around
certain friends? When they were younger and more naïve,
they might have asked us, "Hey, Mom and Dad, what's so
appealing about participating in an activity that completely
contradicts what you say you believe?" But now that they are
solidly in their teen years, they just give us a fist bump and
follow our lead.

Separation of Behaviors, Not Love and Influence

When I think about teaching our kids that it's not okay to
conform to the pattern of the culture, the first passage of

Scripture that comes to mind is 2 Corinthians 6:14–17. In these verses, Paul says:

> Do not be yoked together with unbelievers. For what do righteousness and wickedness have in common? Or what fellowship can light have with darkness? What harmony is there between Christ and Belial? Or what does a believer have in common with an unbeliever? What agreement is there between the temple of God and idols? For we are the temple of the living God. As God has said: "I will live with them and walk among them, and I will be their God, and they will be my people." Therefore, "Come out from them and be separate, says the Lord. Touch no unclean thing, and I will receive you."

It's important to recognize that this call for separation is not a command to segregate ourselves from anyone who does not profess faith in Christ; it's a call to be separate in our actions. Paul cautions about those who worship idols, do wickedness, and are involved in unclean things. But he does not call us to separate ourselves from those we are called to love, serve, and reconcile to Christ. Our commitment to love and serve those who don't know our Lord is a far cry from embracing as our own all the ways of the world.

What about Those Gray Areas?

A kid once said to me, "Nowhere in the Bible does it say not to go to an R-rated movie!" I had to suppress a laugh before saying, "Okay, you've got me there, but I think lust is covered quite well." But what do we do about those morally gray areas of life? And before you go get all fundamentalist on me, there are gray areas! Believers of goodwill and solid faith and commitment do disagree on some ethical choices: consumption of alcohol or getting a tattoo are examples. How do we help our kids navigate those morally gray choices they often face?

Let's turn once again to the apostle Paul. A big stink was apparently going on in the church at Corinth, and it all centered around a rump roast. This is my paraphrase, but the story goes something like this. Many of the believers in Corinth came to Christ from a pagan religion in which all the animals that had been sacrificed in the temple to the pagan god would be sold in the pagan temple butcher shop. Well, the Christians in Corinth who had not come out of that pagan religion loved shopping at the pagan temple butcher shop because the rump roast was at least fifty cents cheaper than the meat in other markets. The Christians who had not come out of the pagan religion did not see anything wrong with buying this meat that had been sacrificed to an idol. They felt a freedom to buy the meat if they wanted to. However, the believers who had come out of that pagan religion considered buying meat that had been sacrificed to a pagan god to be a great sin and judged those who did buy the meat harshly. So now we're caught up on the big stink that Paul had to address.

His response was so true to his character. He said in 1 Corinthians 8:9–13:

> Be careful, however, that the exercise of your rights does not become a stumbling block to the weak. For if someone with a weak conscience sees you, with all your knowledge, eating in an idol's temple, won't that person be emboldened

to eat what is sacrificed to idols? So this weak brother or sister, for whom Christ died, is destroyed by your knowledge. When you sin against them in this way and wound their weak conscience, you sin against Christ. Therefore, if what I eat causes my brother or sister to fall into sin, I will never eat meat again, so that I will not cause them to fall.

It turns out that the issue had nothing to do with whether they should eat the meat. The issue was that if what they were doing was causing a fellow brother or sister, *for whom Christ died*, to stumble, then they should never eat meat again. Think of it this way: if we do something that causes one of our brothers or sisters in Christ to stumble, our sin is a lack of love for them, not whatever we are doing.

My youngest daughter, on her eighteenth birthday, made it known that she wanted to get her belly button pierced. Fighting the urge to yell at her that she was crazy, I stated, "Hey, sweetie. You have been a phenomenal young woman. You've lived an incredible life that has honored God, so if you want to get your belly button pierced, you have earned the right to do that. If you can do that without hurting your witness, go right ahead. If you can pierce your belly button without causing guys to focus on your lower midsection, your erogenous zone, have at it. Oh, and one more thing. If you decide to do this, I just want you to know that I will go with you and have your mother's name and likeness tattooed on my backside, and you will have to stand there and witness the whole thing." I'm still not sure why, but she decided not to go through with it.

Of course, our kids also face obvious moral decisions, like getting drunk, doing drugs, or having sex outside of marriage. The way to handle these situations is biblically quite clear. But for all the less obvious situations, we can let Paul's instruction to the church at Corinth be our guide. It's a simple but profound principle: we must be careful of the effect of what we do and where we go. If our actions cause another brother or sister in Christ to stumble, then we should not engage in those activities—no matter who's going or how much fun it might be.

All I Want Is for My Child . . .

So what should we desire for our children? If not to be happy, then what? Simply put, one of God's main goals in life is for us not to be happy but to have joy! Joy is different from happiness. Happiness is temporal, fleeting. It can't be the ultimate goal for our kids, because it's like a vapor; it's like trying to hold sand between our fingers or, as Solomon put it, "a chasing after the wind" (Eccles. 1:14). But joy is a completely different concept. Joy is not the result of our circumstances—it is derived from the indwelling of the Holy Spirit in our lives. It delivers a constant state that transcends circumstances. That's why James could tell us to count our life's trials as pure joy. Not because they are fun and produce happiness but, rather, because they are no fun at all yet produce perseverance and spiritual maturity. That is precisely why Paul writes in Romans 5:3–5, "Not only so, but we also glory in our sufferings, because we know that suffering produces perseverance; perseverance, character; and character, hope. And hope does not put us to shame, because God's love has been poured out into our hearts through the Holy Spirit, who has been given to us."

Paul said something else in his letter to the church at Philippi that I think sums up what the true goal for our children should be. Instead of emphasizing to our children the importance of getting into a good college or making a ton of money someday or fitting in with their friends now, we should be diligent to raise them in such a way that they may "become blameless and pure, 'children of God without fault in a warped and crooked generation,'" in which they will shine like stars in the universe (Phil. 2:15).

Five Practical Changes You Can Make Today

1. Let your child see you model sacrifice and serve others. Intentionally, do not always give your child what they want. Begin to train them to understand that their wants and desires are not the most important things on earth.

2. Help your child evaluate their peer-influenced choices, not in terms of whether a choice makes them feel good but, rather, whether their choice will cause a weaker brother or sister in Christ to stumble. Help them develop the habit of thinking about whether their decision will hurt their witness for Christ, and if the answer is yes, then to have the ability and determination to show restraint.

3. Begin teaching and demonstrating to your child that we can be people's friends and not judge them in the least or participate in all they do. Our separation is in our behavior or actions, not in our love for and relationship with our friends whom Christ has called us to reach.

4. Encourage and celebrate the differences in choices between your child and their secular friends. Teach and demonstrate to them that being different is okay. Jesus was different! Our difference is a good thing, an honorable thing. It's nothing to be ashamed of.

5. When your child gets upset about not being able to do something or go somewhere, lead them into a discussion of how our "want tos" naturally change once we truly follow Christ. Fight the feeling to judge them, and just listen. Understand their need to be accepted, but encourage the idea that God is not a cosmic party pooper who only cares about how miserable He can make us. He loves us and knows what's best for us—even though we may disagree with His decision.

6

Prioritize Family Relationships

> *Robert and Jill were in a counseling session talking about
> their sixteen-year-old son, Chad, and his defiant behavior,
> but it soon became evident that their marriage was in a
> stressful state as well. Jill conceded, "I'm the one with him all
> day long, so I'm always the heavy. But you're right, Chad
> and I do need to work on our relationship." Robert inter-
> rupted and flatly stated, "You don't have a relationship with
> Chad. You guys never speak to each other or communicate
> at all. In fact, did you know he's had a girlfriend for over
> a month? That he didn't make the robotics team? Or how
> about this? Did you know he was offered weed for the first
> time . . ." You could tell by the quiver in Robert's voice that
> he was getting emotional. ". . . and our boy said no." In re-
> sponse to all Robert's questions, Jill reluctantly had to admit
> that she didn't know. She had to admit that she didn't have
> much of a relationship with her son at all.*

f you were to dig just a little deeper into Jill's story, you'd
find that Jill and Chad had struggled in their relationship

for a long time. Chad's biological father and Jill had gone through an ugly divorce ten years earlier and were barely on speaking terms at the time of our session. Jill disliked her ex-husband because she felt he was selfish, rude, and narcissistic; she also felt Chad was the spitting image of his father both physically and in his personality. So why was her relationship with Chad always on edge? I think many in the psychology field might call it transference. Chad reminded her so much of her ex that she inadvertently imposed her feelings toward that ex onto the son who so closely resembled him. With this revelation and a ton of hard work, it wasn't long before Jill began to see that she was, in fact, taking out a lot of her past disdain toward her ex on her son. Things began to improve for that family, but their situation emphasizes the importance of prioritizing family relationships.

The lack of solid, trusting relationships between parents and kids today is becoming an epidemic. It might take a patient weeks to get in to see a family counselor because the counselor's schedule is just so full. At our offices, many kids and adults come for counseling for anxiety and depression issues, but the number of those clients pales in comparison to the number of parents who come in due to family relationship problems. When I speak to audiences about parent/child relationships, it never fails to generate a sizable queue of people waiting to ask questions. People are eager for any advice to help them deal with what they see as a desperate relational situation with their children.

Why are the relationships with our kids so important? What's causing these problems? And how do we begin to repair what's broken? That's what this chapter is all about.

Why Are Relationships So Important?

I realize that I may be preaching to the choir. You may already know this, but Christianity is significantly different from other religions of the world in that it is not based on a collection of beliefs and cultural systems that enable people to find their way to God and learn the pathway to heaven. No, Christianity is substantively different. It is the story of God reaching down to humankind. God loving us. God finding us. God dying for us. And for what? That's right, a relationship. The apostle John put it this way: "For God so loved the world that he gave his one and only Son, that whoever believes in him shall not perish but have eternal life" (John 3:16). So Scripture tells us that God loved and gave because He wanted to be reconciled with us and be with us forever. He desperately wants a relationship with His children. That's why relationships with our children are so important, because we have been created by God to thrive and rely on relationships. Throughout His life, Jesus modeled their importance. So how important are our relationships with our kids? Our heavenly Father considers them important enough for Jesus, His precious Son, to be butchered on a cross so that you and I can have an enduring, intimate connection with Him.

In his book *Concentric Circles of Concern*, W. Oscar Thompson writes that *relationship* is the most important word in the English language.[1] Why would he make such a bold, declarative statement? Well, without relationship, there is no community, no culture, no science, no learning, no artistic expression, no music, no entertainment, no friendship, no family, no faith, no . . . love. Without relationship, we have virtually nothing that is of worth to us as human beings.

To that point, have you ever noticed that music can transport you mentally and emotionally? I can hear a song on the radio or on my phone and be taken back to an exact time and place. That's what happened some years back when I was driving to a speaking event and "If You Leave Me Now" by Chicago came on the radio. I was transported back to high school, when that song would play incessantly on the jukebox at the city pool, where I happened to be a lifeguard. What a great time in my life. I was young and handsome, and my stomach was still an internal organ. I can remember that glorious feeling of being able to look down and see my feet. Ah, those were the days.

But instead of having this wonderful feeling of nostalgia as I was driving down the highway, I felt empty, a gnawing sense of incompleteness that was difficult to understand. Why was this melancholy hanging around, when everything in my life was so good at the time this song was popular? I continued to ponder this over as I drove the next several miles, and then it dawned on me. My kids. My kids didn't exist on the planet at that time. My life did not contain those closest to me when I was that young. The thought of a world without them in it struck me as hollow and unfulfilling.

Have you noticed that you feel out of place, out of sorts, and out of touch when your relationships with your kids are rocky? We miss the familiarity healthy relationships with our kids bring, and all is not right with the world until those relationships are restored. We need to focus on the relationships with our kids because we need those relationships. We are like Christ when our hearts reach out to touch the hearts of our children with love and intimacy. We need the love and intimacy, and they need them too. We can almost feel the joy of God when we enter into authentic, true relationships with them.

The Roadblocks to Relationships with Our Kids

Over the years as a family therapist, I've had the opportunity to examine, in detail, parents who have strained relationships with their children. If we were to gather all those parents together to see what lies at the heart of those relational problems, three particular issues would become clear.

Personality Differences

Have you ever had one of those relationships with your child? Due to no one's fault in particular, there just always seems to have been a rift between you two. You don't know why they get under your skin. They can get you to argue at the drop of a hat. They can get on your last nerve without even trying. And try as you might, you simply don't get where they're coming from. Your other children don't cause you to feel this way, but this one . . .

Relationship differences come in all shapes and sizes. A child may remind you of a parent you didn't like or, as mentioned previously, an ex-spouse. Or the problem may be that the child is exactly like you, which often breeds discontent. A good portion of our personalities are established at birth. Kids have proclivities in attitude and actions that are "hardwired" in them, so to speak, from the moment they hit fresh air. Sometimes those hardwired aspects of their personalities don't always mesh easily with the hardwired aspects of their parents' personalities. As Shakespeare's Hamlet once put it, "Aye, there's the rub." We've all known people whose personalities drive us crazy, right? Their mere presence can cause our blood pressure to spike. Well, if this isn't your reality, could you imagine if that was true of you and your child? Some parents are at a relational disadvantage with their child right from the very beginning.

Personality differences are difficult to manage, because many times they are covert instead of overt. The reason for the distance between you and your child is not easily understood. The cause is not readily identified, so a remedy is often not even pursued. A feeling can develop that makes you think, *Oh well, I guess this is just the way it's going to be between me and my child.* You may reluctantly accept this distance as a permanent aspect of your relationship with your child, but this is a mistake you don't have to make.

Living Parallel Lives

The family is up and at 'em at 5:30 a.m. every morning. Mom's setting the cereal boxes out on the table; Dad's stuffing a cinnamon roll in his mouth as he utters a garbled "good-bye" before speed-walking out the door to head to the office. Mom yells at the sophomore girl to get in the car or she's going to be late for swim practice; then she hollers at the boys to get ready because she will be back in exactly twenty minutes to drive them to school. She does make it back, just a little more than five minutes late, but manages to get them both to school before the bell rings . . . then she races off to her own job. After school is equally hectic, with kids being dropped here, parents attending a meeting there, everyone eating different fast-food meals at separate times.

Dad gets home and goes to work in his study, Mom labors to get the household chores done for the day, and each kid is in their bedroom, supposedly working on homework, but most of their time is spent texting and Snapchatting on their phones. Add this typical day to a bunch more and you get a typical week, a typical month, a typical year, a typical life of a twenty-first-century Christian family.

And we wonder why we don't have the type of relationships with our kids that we would like. Because this problem of living parallel lives simply follows the path of least resistance, it is easy to get sucked into. If we are not intentional about sharing our lives in a way that we know about, discuss, share, listen to, and understand the day-to-day joys and struggles of our children, then they will sail through those years in our homes and then go off to college, and we will have been like ships passing in the night.

Having Other Priorities

I had a pastor tell me once that he admired the way some men were able to have such great relationships with their children. He reminded me, however, that being a successful pastor at a large church takes a great deal of work and skill. You have to be able to raise money, build new buildings, write books, and produce big attendance numbers on a weekly basis. Then he said these devastating words: "But, hey, to be successful in this life, you have to sacrifice something, right? For me, I guess it was my kids."

To say the least, you wouldn't expect a pastor to utter those words, but you wouldn't really expect any Christian parent to express them either, right? Yet the reality of this statement is being played out in homes all across this country. Our relationships with our children are suffering because we, as parents, have other priorities. I know we'd like to convince ourselves that everything we do is for our families, but if we were just slightly honest with ourselves, we'd have to admit that we are simply trying to justify our success-driven life choices. I will guarantee that no matter what our children may say now, the truth be known, they would much rather have a close, intimate relationship with their mom and dad than a big house, a luxury car, all the latest clothes, a huge TV, or an all-expenses-paid college education. A child may think these things are important when they're young and their brains are underdeveloped, but we're supposed to be the adults. We should know that if we were left with one hour to live, we would not choose to spend time with any one of those "things." We would want to spend every last second with the people who are the unquestioned priorities in our lives, the people who are truly precious to us—our spouse and children.

Steps to Refocusing on Relationships

There are obviously many other roadblocks to healthy family relationships, but if we could just make headway toward solving these three, we would be light-years ahead of where we are now. So let's take an in-depth look at each of these roadblocks and see how we can remove them from our homes for good.

Overcoming Personality Differences

Perhaps you are familiar with Gary Chapman's bestselling book, *The 5 Love Languages*. If not, the premise is that we communicate love in five different "languages," and if we love our spouse in a language different from their own, then we feel as though we are loving them, but they do not feel it. If we show them love through acts of service, when their love language is words of affirmation, it's very frustrating for both parties. The overarching concept of the book is this: our job is not simply to love our spouse but to make sure our spouse feels loved by us. Big difference. It is our job to change the way we love our spouse to make sure they feel loved by us.

This is the exact concept we need to apply to our relationships with our kids. When we have a child with a personality that agitates us, we have to change our parenting approach to make sure they feel loved by us. Yes, our personalities may clash, but again, we're the adult. It's our job to understand this inherent conflict and then change the way we would normally interact with them in order to make sure they feel loved by us. I am sure you're thinking, *You have no idea what I'm living with. No one could possibly live in peace with this kid!* I know how you may feel, but as Jesus put it in Matthew 5:43–47:

> You have heard that it was said, "Love your neighbor and hate your enemy." But I tell you, love your enemies and pray for those who persecute you, that you may be children of your Father in heaven. He causes his sun to rise on the evil and the good, and sends rain on the righteous and the unrighteous. If you love those who love you, what reward will you get? Are not even the tax collectors doing that? And if you greet only your own people, what are you doing more than others? Do not even pagans do that?

Our children, of course, are not our enemies, but we are not given an "out" to accept strained relationships with them simply because their personalities conflict with ours.

Should we discipline them when their behavior warrants it? Absolutely. We are not, however, allowed to hold a grudge against one of our kids simply because their personality grates on us. Remember, we shouldn't hold it against our child simply because they have a personality that tends to irritate us. Our goal is to discipline behavior, not personality.

Making Separate Lives One Life

Many of us enjoy the stage in life when our children get old enough to have some independence. We don't have to pick up after them constantly or entertain them, and we finally have a small slice of time all to ourselves. This tiny glimpse of freedom, however, comes with a price. If a child is allowed to assume all the distance and independence they desire, this way of life can become extreme and permanent. Because our children are no longer pursuing our attention and interaction doesn't mean our relationships with them have to suffer. When our children hit early adolescence and begin to pull away from us, we must begin to pursue them. Gone are the days when our children run to us; now we have to run to our children.

Teenagers basically have two jobs to accomplish during their adolescent years: form their own identity (separate from their parents) and establish their independence (apart from their parents). This individualization is healthy, normal, appropriate, and desirable. We should want this to happen. What's the alternative? Having a forty-year-old child living upstairs? No thank you. But as is true in all other aspects of parenting, we must monitor this behavior to make sure it stays within healthy boundaries. Our relationships with our teenagers should contain a developmentally appropriate distance, not the Grand Canyon. True, the older they get the more "space" we give them, yet we must remain vigilant that the once-healthy space does not morph into a chasm without our even recognizing it.

We must remain in constant communication but not demand that they communicate on our time schedule. Don't judge their desire to connect by their grumbled response to the question "How was your day, honey?" I always tell parents that communication with their adolescent child is best accomplished by being in their presence as much as possible—or as much as they can stand. You have to be in the room when *they* feel like talking, because knowing them involves so much more than simply knowing their schedule.

Kids tend not to speak to their parents for two reasons: fear and frustration. One, they fear their parents' response; second, they feel like they are not heard or taken seriously, so they feel frustrated. There is a truism in counseling that goes like this: "You train people how to treat you." Answer this honestly. Have you taught your child not to share personal issues with you? When they did, did you try to teach them a lesson? Point out how stupid their thinking was? When they confessed a poor decision, did you blow up and show anger and disappointment? The reason our kids don't share more of their lives with us may be looking back at us in the mirror. Don't get me wrong, we are still their parents, and we need to enforce boundaries with appropriate consequences, but we can do that without damaging our relationships in the process. Because enforcing boundaries is not about our anger and frustration. It is simply a matter of doing what we said we would do, being kind and loving in the process. Open and honest communication is the key to several individuals in a home living one life together as a family.

Research tells us that we have an imbalanced view of communication. We usually assume communication means we tell people things so they have information they need. Authentic communication, however, is a two-way street. That means listening is just as important as talking. In a study I did a few years under the Barna Group umbrella in which we studied the practices that enabled parents to raise godly children, one of the most important findings was that parents need to talk less and listen more.[2] Not because the parents don't have useful wisdom to share that would benefit their children but because they cannot be sure which nuggets of wisdom are appropriate to share if they don't truly grasp what's going on in the minds and hearts of their children. Listening also reflects our respect for the other person, which then makes them more open to what we have to say. Until they believe they have been heard, we are not likely to be heard.

One final thought regarding the challenge of truly connecting with our kids. Recent research has shown that one-third of all parents feel guilty for not spending enough time with their children. But the same research also revealed what many parents have learned the hard way: connecting at a deep level with our children is often not so much about carving out more time for them as it is about making the time provided really count.[3] This is more than the old quantity versus quality time debate. Healthy families enjoy a sufficient quantity of time spent together while using that time, regardless of its duration, to facilitate a high-quality shared experience. So the core issue in this shift is not necessarily to apportion gobs of additional time to family relationships as much as it is to be truly present and invested in our children when we have those times together.

Rearranging Our Priorities

Prioritizing is going to be difficult. We're not asking you to change something you casually care about. We're asking you to make a major shift in your priorities. By definition, priorities are the most important things in your life. To ask someone to take something that is supremely important to them and exchange it with something else is . . . well, problematic, to say the least.

Let's begin by saying that it is misguided to view Satan as having horns and a bifurcated tail. The best, most accurate image of the Evil One, in fact, is as an old man, in a trench coat, out behind an adult bookstore. Why? Because Satan is a pervert. He perverts things; that's what he does. Keep in mind that to pervert something is to distort or corrupt it from its original purpose or meaning. I think that's what Paul had in mind when he said in 2 Corinthians 11:14, "And no wonder, for Satan himself masquerades as an angel of light." The Deceiver takes good things, appropriate things, and perverts them to our detriment. He takes the good and noble and perverts them into a force of destruction in our lives and in the lives of our families.

For the sake of clarity, please realize there is nothing wrong, whatsoever, with working at a good, high-paying job; living in a nice house; having an expensive car; and raising kids who make straight As and excel at every sport they try. However, Satan can and does take these good things and perverts them to his purposes. For instance, he makes money our god, our kids' success the foundation of our own self-worth, and keeping up with the Joneses our main obsession.

So we're asking you not to get rid of these good things in your life but simply to rearrange your priority list. A tweak, so to speak (rhyme absolutely intended). I think my high school football coach got it right when he told us, "Boys, to have a successful, winning football team, I just need you to rank your priorities in this order: faith, family, and then football. If you commit your life to God first, then commit to your family, football will take care of itself." Parents, if we put God first in our lives, followed by our families, then all the other issues will take care of themselves.

The great "priority" verse in the Bible is found in Jesus's Sermon on the Mount, as the Lord is discussing all the things the believers were worrying about. Clothes, food, and shelter topped the list of anxiety-producing issues in the lives of first-century Christians. Jesus told them plainly not to worry about those things. Pagans, nonbelievers, worry about such things. As a follower of Christ, one who professes faith in Him, we instead should "seek first his kingdom and his righteousness, and all these things will be given to [us] as well" (Matt. 6:33).

Parents—that is the tweak you need. It doesn't get any clearer. Our lives, our careers, our possessions, our children's academic and athletic achievements should all reflect this one simple priority. As a family, we are to seek first Christ and His kingdom, and everything else we consider to be so important will be taken care of according to His will, not ours. Have you heard it said, "Don't sweat the small stuff, and it's all small stuff"? Well, from a biblical perspective, "Don't sweat anything that is not about the kingdom of Christ, and nothing this world has to offer is about the kingdom."

Relationships are everything in a family. Create and sustain strong, healthy ones and your family will thrive and be in a position to impact this culture for His kingdom. In the next chapter, we will discuss several parenting strategies that have a huge negative impact on those relationships.

Five Practical Changes You Can Make Today

1. Honestly assess your relationships with your kids. Are any of them strained due to personality differences? Do you, in any way, treat one child differently from the others? Do you seem to lose your temper more quickly with one child than with the others? Then, and this is the best part, have your spouse answer these questions for you. They may have a more insightful assessment than you could determine on your own.

2. This is going to take some time, but arrange one-on-one time with each of your children on a regular basis. Go do something they enjoy doing. Try to step out of your role as mentor, coach, and disciplinarian. Simply hang with them, listen, and fight the urge to teach them or give advice. Your job on these outings is simply to laugh, listen, and love on your child. Also, make time on a daily basis to be with your children. Spend some time with them doing homework, playing video games, or just watching TV. Be present when they decide they'd like to talk.

3. Teach your children that it's okay for them to talk to you without fear of your response. They might not like the consequences, but they should not fear your response. Let them know you love and care for them, and thank them for trusting and sharing with you. They'll understand your duty to discipline if they know that love is behind it, not anger or seeming retribution.

4. Change your weekly calendar to reflect the wisdom of Matthew 6:33. Assess whether your kids really need to be in all the activities they participate in. Do your kids' calendars reflect Matthew 6:33? Then take a hard, honest look at your own calendar. Does where you spend your time reflect Matthew 6:33? If you answer no to either of these questions, then, together with your spouse, decide what needs to change and use the time gained to let more of God in.

5. At least once a month, do something together as a family. It doesn't have to be expensive, but it does have to put you all together in one place at the same time, sharing an activity or experience. And wherever you go and whatever you do, make sure to include built-in downtime. Allow for moments to just sit, talk, and share one another's lives.

7

Reject Destructive Parental Behaviors

Anger, Guilt, and Shame

Troy and Linda brought in their fifteen-year-old son, Justin, for counseling because they had received a phone call that he had been caught making out with his girlfriend in the school parking lot. FYI, he went to a local Christian high school. They wanted this first counseling session to include them as well, so I sat down with all three of them together. I had no more gotten all the legalities out of the way before both parents began to launch verbal missiles at their son. To say that they were livid would be an understatement. Here is a snippet of their lecture: "We didn't raise you this way! We are so very disappointed in you. Your teachers are disappointed, and you know what? God is even more disappointed in you! You're always talking at youth group and singing in the worship band, but is this really a reflection of your faith? What do you think all those kids at church are going to say when they hear about this? I never thought

> *a child of ours would turn out to be such a hypocrite and*
> *bring this kind of shame on this family!" And Troy put the*
> *vitriolic icing on this ironic cake when he closed by saying,*
> *"I've never been so ^%&*#@# disappointed in my life."*

That was quite a meeting I had with Troy and Linda. These parents were able to work into a single two-minute tirade all the negative parenting behaviors we will discuss in this chapter. And they did it all without having to take more than a couple of breaths. That one session contained enough irony to fill a Monty Python skit (please tell me you know what that is). I would say that I was, in fact, the only one in that room who was *not* a hypocrite, but that would, of course, be hypocritical (not to mention ironic). To enact the changes we feel are necessary for our families to succeed in an increasingly secular culture, we discussed in the last chapter the need to establish and maintain solid and loving relationships with our kids. This chapter explores some of the most destructive forces that lead to broken relationships in the home. Christ-honoring relationships are essential for our families, and eliminating these forces is essential to achieving that goal.

Parental Parasites

They say everything is bigger in Texas—and that includes the ticks. Those little bloodsuckers are not just a painful addition to all our outdoor activities; they can carry several very serious diseases as well, including Lyme disease and Rocky Mountain spotted fever. You don't notice the ticks when they first attach to you; you notice much later, when it's too late and the potential damage has already been done. In this chapter, we are going to look at two relationally deadly parasites that can attach themselves to parents in such a subtle way that the parents may not even know it. These parasites can suck the lifeblood right out of a family, and the members don't realize the damaging consequences until much later, when the damage has already been done.

Parasite #1: Parental Anger

I believe that parental anger, especially the parental anger outburst, is the single most destructive force within a family. Not anger in general, but parental anger. Do kids get angry? Of course they do. But they are kids; kids throw tantrums. That's what a child with less than a fully developed brain does. We, however, are adults. We are supposed to have outgrown that type of childish behavior. We, the parents, are supposed to have our acts together so our children trust us implicitly as the rock they can rely on to protect them from the storms of life. We are not supposed to become an actual verbal and emotional storm ourselves.

I wish I could tell you this issue is not as bad inside the Christian community as it is outside of it, but that doesn't seem to be the case. For example, recently a couple sat in my office discussing their sixteen-year-old son and his defiant behavior. After some back and forth about just how horrible his son's behavior really was, the dad finally, reluctantly, confessed, "Okay, I admit that sometimes I get so frustrated with him that I do raise my voice. I know I shouldn't do that." The mom, with a shocked expression on her face, looked across at her husband and said, "Honey, you do more than raise your voice. Just this morning, you screamed at our son and called him a fat, worthless piece of @#$%!"

The father is an elder at his church, leads a small group in their home, and sponsors every youth event he can. Yet in a moment of uncontrolled anger, he let loose a verbal assault that will reside in that young boy's heart for a lifetime. How could he do it? In a word, he felt *justified*.

I had another dad in my office with anger issues that were deemed "out of control," so I asked him a few questions.

"Hey," I said, "if your ten-year-old daughter, Emily, said or did something very offensive to you, would you ever ball up your fist and hit her in the face just as hard as you could?"

"No! Absolutely not!" he said.

"But, I mean, what if she said something really bad?"

"Are you crazy? There is no way I would ever do that!" he replied.

"So what you're saying is that there is no scenario in which you would ever hit your child in the face as hard as you could. That act would *never* be justified. So, Mr. Out of Control, you actually do have control. You do have a line that you will not cross, no matter what. What we have to do is move that uncrossable, absolutely-no-justification-to-ever-cross line back from hitting your child in the face to screaming, cursing, and name-calling, because those behaviors are totally unjustifiable as well."

I think most parents who have anger outbursts would agree with this dad. They could never just haul off and smack their child in the face—well, some could, but most couldn't. That would never be justified, under any circumstances. But scream at them, embarrass them, degrade them, browbeat them, cuss at them? Those things they feel completely justified doing.

120

But we are not justified in selfishly dumping our rage on our children, no matter what they did. Uncontrolled anger is a destructive psychological force, which is why God's Word is anything but silent on the subject. One of the most famous verses about anger in the Bible is James 1:19, which says, "My dear brothers and sisters, take note of this: Everyone should be quick to listen, slow to speak and slow to become angry." Why would the brother of Jesus command us to be slow to anger if we are justified in flying off the handle every time our children disobey us?

Here is a sure sign that you are trying to justify your anger. Have you ever apologized to your child due to an out-of-control anger outburst? You realized your actions were over the top and felt as though you needed to say you were sorry. Offering that apology is great, by the way. Our children need to know that we make mistakes sometimes and that asking forgiveness is the best route to reconciliation. Parental humility is a fantastic quality to exhibit to our kids. However, did you happen to notice if your apology contained a big "but"? You see, there is no "but" in an apology. To apologize for wrong behavior, then follow it with a giant "but" is to, in a not-so-subtle way, place the blame for your bad behavior on someone or something else. This is the same mentality used by men who abuse their wives. They say, "Well, sure I shouldn't have hit you, but, hey, you burned the bacon. What was I supposed to do?" As ridiculous as this sounds, it is really no different than saying, "Honey, I shouldn't have yelled at you like that, *but* you have to obey me when I ask you to do something." As parents, we must own our negative behaviors and make no excuses for them.

I'm not sure we actually understand the importance Scripture places on avoiding anger outbursts. Take a look at the company anger keeps in Paul's letter to the church in Galatia: "The acts of the flesh are obvious: sexual immorality, impurity and debauchery; idolatry and witchcraft; hatred, discord, jealousy, *fits of rage*, selfish ambition, dissensions, factions and envy; drunkenness, orgies, and the like. I warn you, as I did before, that those who live like this will not inherit the kingdom of God" (Gal. 5:19–21, emphasis added). Did you realize that a fit of rage was lumped in with heavy-hitting sins like witchcraft and orgies? That was done for a reason. Anger can leave emotional scars that last a lifetime. That old saying "Sticks and stones may break my bones, but words will never hurt me" might be the dumbest statement ever made.

But not only are rage and anger outbursts destructive to our relationships with our kids, but they can also negatively impact how children on the receiving end of such ugliness view their heavenly Father. When our children are little, their entire concept of God is wrapped up in their view of their parents. They tend to equate our attributes with the attributes of God. If we are loving and kind, then their view of God skews toward Jesus's love and forgiveness. But if we regularly engage in episodes of rage and anger, then they could very easily view God in the Old Testament sense of "destroy-every-man-woman-child-gerbil-cat-dog-and-spider-monkey-in-that-pagan-city-sayeth-the-Lord-God-Almighty" sort of way. Our behavior impacts our kids, since their view of Christ is reflected through us.

Parasite #2: Guilt and Shame

We all want to motivate our kids to make the right choices. We try incentives, consequences, modeling, and reasoning, and when all else fails, we use guilt and shame as motivational tools. Why do we do this? For many of us, it is because that was how we were parented. One or both of our parents would shame us or "put us on a guilt trip" after we did something wrong. One mother told her son in my office, "I can't believe you made your father and me look like such idiots! Do you not love us at all? Do you know this could cost your father his job? His job! He's the principal of the school and what you did reflects on his leadership! If he gets fired, young man, it will be squarely on you! I . . . I don't even know who you are anymore."

Believe me, I understand completely. We want our children to feel remorse, to understand the seriousness of what they have done. We want them to get it, and if they're not going to come to that conclusion on their own, we feel it's our job to help them along.

We desire for our children to connect the dots and see the big picture. Their actions seem so mindless at times, like their brains just fell out of their heads. We feel compelled to make sure they do understand, to make sure they see their inconsistency and completely grasp the full impact of their actions. We want to use each behavioral episode as a teachable moment in their lives. Yes, I get it and I do see where you, as a parent, are coming from. You have the best intentions, but the road to hell is paved with good intentions.

Remember, we are to be to our children as God is to us. And when we look at Scripture, we are hard-pressed to see Jesus use guilt and shame to motivate people. He met and interacted with all sorts of sinners, and He encouraged them, corrected them, guided them, warned them, accepted them, forgave them, and loved them. But other than with the Pharisees, He never shamed, condemned, or used guilt as a motivator. Nowhere in our parental model of discipline should we find guilt and shame. According to 2 Corinthians 5:18, "All of this is from God, who reconciled us to himself through Christ and gave us the ministry of reconciliation." Yes, Paul is referring to reconciling a lost world back to Him, but it doesn't stop there. The main goal of disciplining our kids should be to reconcile them back to their heavenly Father, not to wound them with guilt and shame. In fact, Paul further emphasizes the point in Romans 8:1 when he writes, "Therefore, there is now no condemnation for those who are in Christ Jesus." If God does not condemn us, then we have to avoid condemning our children with the brutal weapons of guilt and shame. Brennan Manning, in his amazing book *The Ragamuffin Gospel*, states, "When we wallow in guilt, remorse, and shame over real or imagined sins of the past, we are disdaining God's gift of grace."[1] We, as believing parents, certainly don't want to be the source of our children learning to disdain the grace of God.

But what if our kids don't get it? What if they don't connect the dots and see the big picture? We're their parents, right? Isn't that our job? Good questions. Because you're right—it is essential that our kids understand the implications of their actions, spiritual and otherwise. They need to feel the pain and grasp the spiritual significance. Teaching them that is an important job—but it's not yours alone. Repeat after me: "There is a Holy Spirit, and I am not Him." There is a big difference between the conviction of the Holy Spirit and the guilt that many parents dump on their kids. The conviction of the Holy Spirit is steeped in the love of the

Father and leads to repentance and a closer walk with Him. Guilt is a tool in the hands of the Adversary, who pushes us away from God while building shame and resentment—two feelings that quickly corrode relationships.

Kids don't grow up and go to counseling because they did wrong and their parents lovingly molded and corrected them in an attempt to bring them back into a close relationship with Christ. They end up in counseling, with a very skewed view of God, because of memories of their parents saying to them, "I'm so ashamed of you. How can you even call yourself a Christian? How could you do this to our family? If this family falls apart, it's going to be your fault. How could you do this to me? You should be ashamed of yourself! There is no way that you could be a child of mine. Your father left because of you!" If your desire is to plant permanently within your child long-term anger and resentment, then continue to allow the destructive parasites of guilt and shame to influence your parenting and discipline.

Getting Rid of These Parasites

Remember, your job as a parent is not just to love your child; that's a given. Believe it or not, that's the "easy" part. Your job is to make sure your child feels loved by you. Now, that's vastly more difficult. The problem with getting rid of anger, shame, and guilt is that we not only feel as though they are justified but also believe our way of disciplining our children is the godly, righteous, and Christian thing to do. That's why changing these negative habits is so difficult. It's like we're being asked to go against our commitment to God.

Consider that for a moment. That's why Satan is called the Father of Lies, the Deceiver, with a capital *D*. He has deceived us into thinking that bad is good, and not only good, but holy. Steven Weinberg, Nobel Prize–winning physicist, has said, "There will always be good people doing good things and evil people doing evil things. But for good people to do evil things, that takes religion."[2] That's how, during the Crusades, believers by the thousands thought they were glorifying Christ by killing Muslims; how good, devout people in Salem, Massachusetts, in the late 1600s thought they were honoring God by burning innocent people at the stake for being witches; how present-day Islamic jihadists can fathom that beheading and burning people alive, raping children, and forcing children to murder their own families makes their god happy; how the poor, deluded members of the Westboro Baptist Church think picketing dead soldiers' funerals and making their children carry signs stating that "God hates fags" is honoring to their god; and how we parents can justify belittling, ridiculing, and shaming our kids as somehow within our Christian duty.

Look at what God's Word actually says about our interactions with other people—which, of course, include how we talk to our children:

Ephesians 4:29–32

Do not let any unwholesome talk come out of your mouths, but only what is helpful for building others up according to their needs, that it may benefit those who listen. And do not grieve the Holy Spirit of God, with whom you were sealed for the day of redemption. Get rid of all bitterness, rage and anger, brawling and slander, along with every form of malice.

Be kind and compassionate to one another, forgiving each
other, just as in Christ God forgave you.

Hebrews 3:13
But encourage one another daily, as long as it is called "Today,"
so that none of you may be hardened by sin's deceitfulness.

1 Thessalonians 5:11
Therefore encourage one another and build each other up,
just as in fact you are doing.

We are not saying don't discipline your children. When it
comes to giving consequences for inappropriate behavior, by
doing so, we are fulfilling our mandate as parents before God.
In fact, when we discipline our kids, we are being to them
as God is to us. Hebrews 12:6 tells us plainly that the Lord
disciplines those whom He loves. And we should certainly
do the same. But as you can see from the Scripture above,
our interactions with our children, even during the discipline
process, are to be full of encouragement and redemption, as
opposed to anger and guilt and shame. Believe it or not, I've
sinned a couple of times in my life. And in all those times of
turning my back on my heavenly Father and going my own
way, I have experienced His grace, forgiveness, acceptance,
love, and discipline, but never once have I felt His wrath.
Can our kids say the same about us?

Okay, enough about what we shouldn't do. Let's get down
to how to remove these parasites from our families. I have
always believed there are three big rules in regard to removing
anger, guilt, and shame from the discipline process. These
three rules are easy to write in a book but difficult to do, but,
hey, if good parenting were easy, anyone could do it.

Rule #1: Remember That Your First Response Is Your Worst Response

Adrenaline is a parent's worst enemy. This is the hormone that gets us ready to fight or take flight. And since most parents do not run in fear from their kids, adrenaline pumps us up and readies us to fight them. In the midst of the discipline process, this is the hormone that makes us say what we would otherwise never say and do what we would otherwise never do. When our adrenaline is pumping and our blood pressure is soaring, we are not primed to make rational, level-headed, Christ-honoring decisions. Instead, our minds race to extremes, reflecting the intense nature of our emotional condition. Therefore, removing adrenaline from our parenting is job number one.

So remember, when a discipline crisis hits, the first rule for removing anger, guilt, and shame from the equation is to resist the temptation to go with your initial response.

Rule #2: Bring God into the Situation ASAP

In the midst of a disciplinary conflict with your child, the last thing you want to do is handle it on your own. Instead, your best strategy is to get out of the way and let Jesus flow through you to handle the situation. This is exactly the thought behind Paul's words in Galatians 2:20: "It is no longer I who live, but Christ lives in me" (NASB). Your response will be much more successful and you'll be less prone to mistakes if you bring God into the discipline process at the earliest possible moment, echoing the words of John the Baptist when he said of Jesus, "He must become greater; I must become less" (John 3:30). With that in mind, let me walk you through four steps to calling a STOP to an anger-filled discipline episode.

STOP AND SEPARATE

This step is taken with the knowledge that your first response is your worst response. Your first instinct in the midst of an angry, emotional exchange with a defiant child may be to argue with them, lecture them, or proclaim an immediate discipline decision. These will just make a bad situation intolerable, so you need to create time and space to calm down. Separate yourself from the offending child until your adrenaline rush, and theirs, subsides. This may be difficult when tempers are flaring, but it is essential. I propose using the phrase "I'm calling a stop to this" as a way of signaling that tempers are elevating and that a period of separation is needed. Of course, if you just separate and never come back to the issue, that's called avoidance, which is an unhealthy way of dealing with stressful issues. So limit your stop-and-separate period to no more than thirty to sixty minutes. Then come back together to resume the discussion of the issue.

TONE DOWN THE TENSION

During your separation break, you need to focus on letting the anger out and getting a realistic perspective on the situation. This is the time for you and your spouse to discuss the issue. Or if you're alone with your teen, call your spouse or seek the counsel of other family members or friends. If the anger persists and you just can't seem to calm down, try to "change the channel of your brain" by watching TV or doing some yardwork. Do whatever it takes to focus your mind on something other than your intense feelings toward your child.

Open Your Heart to God

Opening your heart to God is done, of course, through prayer. Pray that God will give you the ability to overcome your feelings of anger. Pray that this event will be a teachable moment for both you and your child. Pray for the wisdom and grace to approach your child with the heart of Christ, not a heart filled with rage or vengeance. And claim the promise from Luke 12:12 in which Jesus instructed His disciples not to worry when they were dragged before any city officials or religious authorities because "the Holy Spirit will teach you at that time what you should say." In the same way, the Holy Spirit will guide you as you speak to your defiant teen in the midst of a discipline episode. That's a promise. After you spend a few minutes seeking the Father's face, you'll find anger no longer has much power over you.

Present Christ to Your Child

God desires more than anything else to be reconciled with your child in a strong, intimate relationship. He loves that child beyond your ability to comprehend and wants to be reunited in a close, personal, intimate relationship. You are an instrument in His hands to accomplish that desire. This discipline event is not about you lowering the boom or making your child regret ever messing with you. It's about your heavenly Father desiring reconciliation with your child and you being His representative in that room to help bring that about.

Remember that STOP is a strategy to bring God into the discipline process, but it can be used in any tension-filled parent-child situation, even outside of a disciplinary conflict. The most important aspect of STOP is ensuring that both parties—parent and child—drop the argument and separate. The rest of the process cannot work if the argument is carried on uninterrupted.

Rule #3: See Discipline as Redemptive, Not Punitive

Seeing discipline as redemptive, not punitive, is a fundamental change in the way most of us view our role in discipline. We learned from a young age that the fear of punishment is the motivating force behind all discipline. This may be true from a child's perspective, but we, as parents, have to aim higher than that.

I can recall one of my clients, a single mom, who did a great job with her two teenagers and provided a perfect example of what we're talking about. Both kids were acting up at a restaurant, and when their mom attempted to correct them, they responded with disrespect. When they all got back in the car, she told the two teens that their behavior was not acceptable and they could expect several specific consequences to be enforced during the coming week. Needless to say, both kids were beside themselves with anger, disgust, and disbelief that their lame mother would respond like this.

When the family arrived home, the two teenagers were instructed to go to their own rooms. Many parents would have just dropped the issue, grateful to go on about their busy day. Not this mom. About an hour later, she went up to see her son. They had a terrific conversation, tears were shed, and she could sense that redemption was present in the room. Then she went to her daughter's room, where she was rebuffed at the door. Yet this determined mom forged ahead and sat next to her daughter on the bed to explain the situation. She tried to paint a picture of why she had made her decision and of how much she loved this girl and her brother—more than either of them could know. Even though this angry young lady refused to allow even a glimmer of kindness to show through her cloak of fury, her mom took courage in knowing that she'd spoken the words her kids needed to hear and set forth the discipline her kids needed to experience—the rest was up to God. What I love about this mom is that she didn't stop at punishment; her focus all along was redemption—and God will honor that commitment.

The parental changes suggested in this book are predicated on a good relationship between the parent and the child. This alone will cause our families to stand out in a world of lessening parental involvement and digital isolation. As mentioned in the last chapter, a relationship is key to implementing all the recommendations you've been reading. We can never emphasize enough that Christ was crucified on a cross to maintain a relationship with us. We must be willing to do whatever it takes to do the same with our children. And "whatever it takes" includes removing anger, guilt, and shame from our parenting repertoire.

Five Practical Changes You Can Make Today

1. Talk with your spouse (or if single, a close friend) about how each of you was parented. Did your parents use

anger, guilt, and shame when they disciplined you? How so? Do you remember how you felt about it? Have those parasites crept into your parenting and discipline? If so, how? Resolve to remove those practices, and develop a specific plan for what alternative measures you will take.

2. What specific steps can you take to remove adrenaline from the discipline process? Are they practical? What obstacles do you feel you will have to overcome?

3. The next time you have to discipline your older child or teen, try sharing with them examples of how you messed up when you were a child. You paid the price and moved on, just like God wants us to do. Sinning doesn't put us on God's naughty list. Paul was a professional Christian persecutor, and look what God did to use him for His glory!

4. Try using the STOP method of removing anger from your discipline. Afterward, talk with your spouse about how it went, and at the appropriate time, ask your child how that discipline episode went. Brainstorm ways to make it go even better next time.

5. Read *The Ragamuffin Gospel* by Brennan Manning. Your concept of the grace of God will be forever changed. Trust me, this newfound view of grace will trickle down into every aspect of your life—especially your parenting.

8

Reject Materialistic Entitlement

It was the Tuesday after Christmas when thirteen-year-old Chris sat in my office fighting back the urge to break down and cry. He would barely respond to my questions about how his Christmas went—whether his older brother and sister made it in from college or if they had a huge meal or if his beloved Texans had won their football game. It wasn't until I got around to asking what presents he got from ol' Saint Nick that we hit on the issue. When I pressed him as to the source of his sorrow, he looked at me with a mix of confusion and contempt. With his bottom lip quivering and a glare in his eye, he stammered, "I didn't get what I told them I wanted! I told them! I even put it on their &^%!@#$ list! Do you know how it's going to look when all my friends come over and I still have my old Xbox? Every one of them got the newest Xbox for Christmas, and now my games are going to look like $#@$! I'm going to look like an idiot!" When I asked him why he thought his parents didn't fulfill his Christmas wish, he shot back with a look of

> *vile disdain. "They told me they couldn't afford it!" he said.*
> *"Can you believe that? That they can't afford it. That's just*
> *%$#+*@!#&!"*

When I was growing up, being sent to my room was a bad thing. I hated it above all other punishments that didn't include my dad's belt. I would be stuck in there for hours, just sitting on my bed, staring at the wall, with nothing more than a few little plastic army men and a Rock'em Sock'em Robots game that I couldn't even play without my brother being the other robot. Today is, well, different. Today, in fact, a typical child's room is an entertainment utopia. They now have HD video game consoles, two-way handheld video communication devices, flat-screen HD televisions with hundreds of channels, and thousands of digital music and movie choices at their fingertips. Twenty years ago, kids would have paid money to spend time in the bedroom of one of today's kids! There is so much. Just so much . . . stuff.

Yet have you noticed that since our children have been given so much, they tend not to appreciate much of anything? The more stuff they have, the less value they place on those items and the less appreciation they have of the cost of all that stuff. Have we, in our zeal to keep up with cultural norms, so inundated our children with material things that they, and we, have come to see these frivolous trinkets as being essential to our children's happiness and positive sense of self-worth? The twenty-first-century Christian family has become overwhelmed with things—things that our children, through the lens of culture, all but demand. To change our direction, it is essential that we grapple with and subdue two of the ugliest roadblocks to a truly Christ-centered home: materialism and entitlement.

What Is and Isn't Materialism

Let's face it. If we compared any of our homes to the average Christian home in the Sudan or Indonesia, every one of us would be considered materialistic. It is easier for a camel to fit through the eye of a needle than for a rich man to make it into heaven, right?[1] That's what Jesus said, but what does that mean exactly? What does it mean to be rich? We tend to consider anyone who has significantly more than we do to be rich. But since many people throughout the world would view virtually all American Christians as rich, does that mean all Americans are doomed to a sinner's hell? Lord, I hope not. Let's look carefully at Paul's words in 1 Timothy 6:9–10: "Those who want to get rich fall into temptation and a trap and into many foolish and harmful desires that plunge people into ruin and destruction. For the love of money is a root of all kinds of evil. Some people, eager for money, have wandered from the faith and pierced themselves with many griefs." So it's not money per se, but the love of money that seems to be the problem.

I have a good friend who is rich by anyone's standards. He told me not too long ago, "You know, last year I made twice as much money as I've ever made before. And I couldn't figure out what I was going to do with all the extra money. I'm not going to raise my standard of living really. I have a nice house, a nice car; I have no need for anything else. Then it hit me. I guess God blessed me with that extra money so He could use that increase for His kingdom." Now, this guy and his wife already give way beyond the standard 10 percent tithe. Apart from that he supports missionaries, ministries, and orphanages all over the world. So he said that he doubled his percentage of giving for the year. Now, more recently, he told me, "You're not going to believe this, but I made twice as much this year as I did last year! I know God said test me and I'll open up the floodgates of heaven, but man did He really mean it. We've got no choice but to double our percentage of giving again!"

Here is a believer with a ton of money, but is he sinning? Or is he using that money, which he considers a blessing from God, for the advancement of His kingdom? The sin of materialism occurs when we consider our material possessions, or money, to be more important than our commitment to Christ, or when things, other than Christ's presence, become the source of our peace and joy. Not only does my friend view his wealth as in no way competing with his faith, but he also sees it as being intrinsically tied to his faith. He considers using his income and all his possessions to advance God's kingdom to be a vital aspect of being a disciple of Christ.

So if simply having money is not the problem, what is the sin of materialism? What seems to be communicated to our Christian kids in our money-oriented culture is a sense that material possessions and the money it takes to buy them are the single most important pursuit of our lives. For example, we communicate this to our kids by the following:

- parents working sixty-hour weeks, at the expense of family, not simply to make ends meet but to afford the bigger house, the fancier car, and the exotic vacation

- parents obsessing over their kids earning the best grades, so they can get into the best colleges, to get the best jobs, to eventually earn the highest salaries
- the family showing the greatest demonstrations of happiness and excitement in relation to the purchase of cars, houses, vacations, or other material things as opposed to seeing one of their child's friends come to Christ, or a donation the family makes to a ministry in need, or helping a needy family
- the family talking frequently in the home about needing money, not having enough money, plans for earning more money, but not discussing the kingdom of God very much

Through how we view and talk about money, we communicate an emphasis on materialism to our children at their peril. The more we knowingly, or unknowingly, call attention to the material things in this life and the thrill that comes from acquiring them, the more a living, vibrant relationship with God is de-emphasized.

When Too Much Gets to Be Too Much

My wife and I were engaged at nineteen years of age. That first Christmas after our engagement, we were asked by her parents to buy "Christmas" for a young nephew who would be staying with them during the holiday. We went to the store, with Beth's mom's credit card, thank heaven, and brought back a ton of toys. Because we were babies ourselves, we didn't know what the appropriate number of Christmas presents should be for a five-year-old, so we wrapped and arranged under the tree a grand total of thirty-five gifts. That's right: thirty-five Christmas presents for one five-year-old boy. When that kid laid eyes on all those gifts that were all for him, to say he was filled with Christmas cheer would be an understatement.

As he began opening them all, however, an interesting thing began to happen. With each new gift he opened, the less time he spent looking at it and the less excitement he showed for it. In fact, he didn't even open all the gifts. Before he was finished unwrapping his bounty, he lost interest and went to play instead. This sweet little boy could be the poster child for what is happening in America today. When our kids have so much, they end up appreciating very little. In his book *Death by Suburb*, David Goetz writes, "Too much of the good life ends up being toxic, deforming us spiritually."[2]

Luke 9 contains a passage that I find fascinating. Right after the exchange in which Jesus asks Peter, "Who do you say I am?" (v. 20), Jesus turns to all the disciples and says, "Whoever wants to be my disciple must deny themselves and take up their cross daily and follow me. For whoever wants to save their life will lose it, but whoever loses their life for me will save it. What good is it for someone to gain the whole world, and yet lose or forfeit their very self?" (vv. 23–25). To my knowledge, this is the first time in the Bible that Jesus addresses the specific issue of what it means to follow Him. When I look at His statement, I think it's astonishing what He didn't say. He didn't say that if you want to follow Him, you must be holy, love God, serve others, help the poor, study His Word, or a whole host of other fantastic attributes of a solid believer. It was as though He was trying to sum up all those qualities into one. And that attribute was to deny yourself.

Parents? How are we doing at teaching our children to deny themselves?

Oscar Wilde once said, "Self-denial is the shining sore on the leprous body of Christianity."[3]

Don't you hate it when a nonbeliever just nails us? The one thing that Jesus felt was so important we in the American church seem to be all but ignoring. Parents today seem confused. Many believe that loving their kids is giving them what they want, making them happy. Where did that idea come from? Giving a child everything they want is not loving them; it's spoiling them. Loving them is giving them what they need, and many, many times what they need is not another "thing." Often what they need is to be told no.

As mentioned earlier, anytime I hear a parent say, "All I want is for my child to be happy," I want to reach across the room and smack them upside the head. What a horrific goal for their child! Do we even understand the implications of that statement? We're basically saying that all we want is for our kids to live a life where every one of their wants and desires is met, a life full of self-gratification and self-indulgence. I know we don't consciously think we're communicating that, but the message is clear. With our actions and attitudes, we're saying, "Child, your wants are preeminent. All other considerations are secondary to fulfilling your desires." No wonder we are taken aback by all the unhappy, self-absorbed kids we see at the grocery store.

In his book *The Christian Atheist*, Craig Groeschel reminds us of the spiritual repercussions of passing on this destructive viewpoint to our kids when he writes, "Think about the implications of this polluted theology: 'I tried religion, but it didn't make me happy. I went to church and it didn't make my life any better. God didn't help me have a better life, so either he failed me or he's not real. Either way, I'm not interested.'"[4] C. S. Lewis echoed the same sentiment in *God in the Dock*: "As you perhaps know, I haven't always been a Christian. I didn't go to religion to make me happy. I always knew a bottle of Port would do that. If you want a religion to make you feel really comfortable, I certainly don't recommend Christianity."[5]

If loving our kids is giving them not what they want but what they need, what is it that our kids need? Here's a partial list, just off the top of my head:

- a close, authentic relationship with Christ
- a close, authentic relationship with parents and family
- a close, authentic relationship with Christian friends
- to be taught respect, discipline, patience, justice, kindness, honesty, self-control, hope, courage, compassion, and love (By love, I mean the ability to put someone else's needs above one's own, the kind of love that sent Christ to the cross.)

Did you notice that not one of these "needs" has a screen, requires batteries, or plugs in? You can't drive them, wear them, play with them, or tweet with them, and not many people would be impressed by them. In fact, many of these needs are hard and painful. That's why our children don't naturally want most of them. It is way too easy to always give our kids what they want. But that's not our job. God put parents in children's lives to ensure these needs are met.

And if we parents would, once again, look in the mirror of our own lives, what kind of example are we setting in regard to materialism? Do we have to have the latest car, newest phone, or whatever the coolest thing is that our friends have? Has Christmas, the ultimate time of giving, become the ultimate time of "getting" for our own families? Are we rolling out of our driveways at 2 a.m. on Black Friday, parking on the sidewalk, and fighting with little old ladies to get our hands on the new, lowest-price video game before they are all gone? Oh, and are we participating in all this materialistic mayhem just hours after we sit around our family feasting table telling one another and God how thankful we are for all our "blessings"? This is an area where we have to focus on getting the plank out of our own eye before addressing the speck in our child's.

The Ugliness of Entitlement

> *A sixteen-year-old girl named Sarah was brought to my office for behavior that was so out of character for her that her parents were stunned. Sarah was a straight-A student, first-chair violinist in the school orchestra, and very active in her youth group. Like most teenagers today, her cell phone was her prized possession, and she used it constantly throughout the day. She didn't get into trouble very often, so when her mom attempted to take away her cell phone as a consequence for missing curfew by a half hour, they were horrified by her response. Sarah literally freaked out, jerked the phone away from her startled mother, reflexively grabbed a knife off the kitchen counter, pointed it at her mother, and screamed, "Stop it! This is MY phone and you have no right to touch my phone! Do you get it? What part of this don't you get?"*

Are Sarah's actions an exaggerated example of the problem? I would hope so. Are her attitude and sense of entitlement an anomaly? The answer is no. In fact, kids' grandiose attitudes of entitlement are so commonplace today that they almost seem to have become the norm. Do any of these phrases ring a bell?

- "Did you snoop through *my* closet?"
- "You have no right to look through *my* phone!"
- "I don't want you in *my* room!"
- "That's *my* backpack! Stop going through *my* stuff!"

Entitlement is the logical conclusion of materialism. When this overabundance of things is given to kids for no reason, they begin to feel, after a while, that they deserve these things or are *entitled* to them. In fact, they can begin to believe that they have a right to all these things and that it's our duty as parents to provide them. And if they don't get the latest iPhone . . . well, perhaps Child Protective Services needs to be called.

If you haven't read any of Simon Sinek's books on leadership, you have missed out. I watched him on the video blog *Inside Quest* recently, and he had these words to say about young people and entitlement:

> Many Millennials grew up being subjected to failed parental strategies. They were told that they were special, all the time. They were told that they could have anything they want in life, just because they want it. Some kids got into honors classes, not because they earned it, but because their parents complained. They got participation medals. Medals for even coming in last. The science is clear that this devalues the medal for those that worked hard and makes the kid who comes in last embarrassed.

... When these kids are then thrust into the real world, in an instant, they learn that they are not special. Their moms can't get them a promotion, you get nothing for coming in last, and you can't just have it because you want it. And in that instant, their entire self-image is shattered.[6]

A child who has been taught an "I am entitled to anything I want" mentality is scary on multiple levels. Not only can this entitlement be seen in their expectation of things, like clothes or electronics, but it can also be seen in the way they expect high grades without the work or to make the varsity team without the work or to secure a spot in the most advanced school band without the work. Situations like these also reveal the kissing cousin of entitlement—Adolescent Narcissistic Fantasy (ANF)—because you'll notice that if they don't make first team or the honor roll, who do they blame? Whose fault is it? That's right, it's the teacher's, the coach's, the director's, or the parent's, but it is certainly not, under any circumstances, their own fault. In their worldview, such failure simply cannot be attributed to them or their actions. A kid with ANF thinks, *Only my friends and I know what is true and right and just and good, and everyone else is an idiot. I'm always picked on, always misunderstood, always the victim, and always unjustly accused.* If Jesus urged His followers to deny themselves, then consider entitlement/ANF to be the exact opposite of that spirit of humility and self-sacrifice.

Nipping Materialism and Entitlement in the Bud

To end this grotesque display of greed, self-indulgence, envy, lack of self-control, selfishness, and lack of generosity in our kids, we must restore a sense of gratitude, appreciation, and thankfulness. We must focus, with laser-like intensity, on these attributes from the crib to the college dormitory. Gratitude, appreciation, and thankfulness must become our priorities in parenting, and this begins with an acknowledgment that Scripture is anything but silent on the issue. Take a look:

Hebrews 13:5

Keep your lives free from the love of money and be content with what you have, because God has said, "Never will I leave you; never will I forsake you."

1 John 2:16

For everything in the world—the lust of the flesh, the lust of the eyes, and the pride of life—comes not from the Father but from the world.

Luke 12:15

Then he said to them, "Watch out! Be on your guard against all kinds of greed; life does not consist in an abundance of possessions."

Luke 12:33–34

Sell your possessions and give to the poor. Provide purses for yourselves that will not wear out, a treasure in heaven that will never fail, where no thief comes near and no moth destroys. For where your treasure is, there your heart will be also.

So as we begin to examine how to change this behavior in our kids, the first thing we are forced to recognize is that a driving force behind these ugly attributes, the singular prominent source from which all this dysfunction flows, is none other than you and me—the parents. We buy the "things" for them; we, time and time again, provide everything they feel entitled to. We're also the ones who sometimes are focused on keeping up with the Joneses as much as, if not more than, our own children.

Set the Example

All of this is a moot point, however, unless we, as parents, begin setting the example for our families that things don't equal happiness. Our children must *see* gratitude, appreciation, and thankfulness in us. Our children must *see* that Christ, family, and people all rank higher on our priority lists than material possessions. Our children must *see* us tithe, *see* us give additional monies to help those in need, and *hear* us minimize the importance of money in day-to-day family conversations. They must *see* our generosity and that we are good stewards of the blessings God has provided, not hoarding them for our own selfish desires.

Clear Up the Concept of Ownership

I cannot count the number of times I have heard a kid in my office complain that their parents went into *their* room without permission and that this breach of privacy was nothing short of a travesty of justice. And many times I'm the one who has to break it to them that their anger is somewhat misguided. That is to say, until they can show a canceled check they wrote to their parents for rent, it is not their room. It is their parents' house; therefore, it is their parents' room. Their parents own it. And not only do they own the room, but they also own the bed the child sleeps in, the dresser their clothes are in, the phone they text on, the laptop they complete homework on, the contacts in their eyes, the braces on their teeth, and the deodorant under their arms. They own it all—lock, stock, and barrel—and they allow their child to utilize these things only out of the goodness and graciousness in their hearts. And just as the Lord giveth and the Lord taketh away, the same holds true with their parents. All those "things" are the parents' to give and take as they see fit. This idea of ownership needs to be made crystal clear to our young ones from an extremely early age.

Clear Up the Difference between Need and Want

One evident sign of immaturity is immediate gratification. Children want what they want and they want it now, while a more mature brain is able to see the benefits of delayed gratification. Most adults can see that delayed gratification may bring pain in the present, but in the long run it will all be to their gain. This is one of the many reasons children need mature adults in their lives—so they can begin to see the bigger picture. To love our children is to meet their needs, all of them, as best we can. And many times we meet their needs by not providing what they want. What they *need* is to do without what "all the other kids have." What they *need* is to learn self-denial, patience, and self-sacrifice. What they *need* is to learn to do without "wants" in order to put other people's needs above their own. What they *need* is to learn to be satisfied with their needs being met, plus maybe a few of their "wants." When our kids demand that all their "needs," plus all their "wants," be met and they aren't, they will likely respond with sullen disappointment, and at worst, they will lash out in anger and selfish outrage—until we teach them a better way.

Change Family Holiday Traditions

One of the most obvious and most impactful strategies you can employ in your family to combat materialism and entitlement in your kids is to change a key ingredient in a couple of your family's holiday celebrations. Thanksgiving and Christmas are the two most cherished holidays of the year, when we as believers are to concentrate on and celebrate the Christian tenets of honest thankfulness and selfless giving. Yet, in our society, these two holidays have become symbolic of gluttony, self-indulgence, and greed.

Beginning this year, start a new Thanksgiving tradition in your home. Before the holiday arrives and you settle in to watch the big NFL game on TV or eat to the point of gastrointestinal distress, spend some time shopping as a family to acquire all the goodies for a second family-sized Thanksgiving feast. Take the kids and all the relatives and fan out in the grocery store and pick out all the food and fixings necessary to make a holiday banquet fit for a king. Then, again as a family, take that meal to a less fortunate family in your community. If you don't know a family in need, the name and address of a needy family can be provided by your church or community organizations. Take the food to the family's home and pray with and for the family. From that Thanksgiving meal forward, your family will have another family to pray for throughout the next year.

When it comes to Christmas, tell your kids you plan to take half of the five hundred dollars set aside to purchase presents for you as a family and purchase Christmas gifts for a needy family with it. Purchase the gifts together, then wrap and deliver them to the needy family. It's critical for the kids to understand that no one in your family is going to get everything on their list, but everyone will get something. But what they will get, which is better than all those gifts put together, is a firsthand knowledge that it truly is more blessed to give than to receive.

This Is a Tough One

Making these changes to squash materialism and entitlement undermine the very essence of American culture and the American dream, yet believers have been making these types of tough choices since the beginning. It is time that Christian families stop accepting secular standards for our homes. Joshua put it this way in Joshua 24:15: "But if serving the LORD seems undesirable to you, then choose for yourselves this day whom you will serve, whether the gods your ancestors served beyond the Euphrates, or the gods of the Amorites, in whose land you are living. But as for me and my household, we will serve the LORD."

Five Practical Changes You Can Make Today

1. Do not pay for kids to do chores. No one gives you twenty bucks to vacuum the living room or do the dishes, so our children shouldn't be paid either. They mow the lawn not for money but because they are members of a family, and we all pitch in to help.

2. Give them an allowance to help them begin to understand how to manage money. No matter the amount, they are to tithe 10 percent, save 10 percent, and the rest is for themselves. As they get older, have them be responsible for things like their entertainment, so if they want to go to the movies with friends, then they need to budget their money accordingly.

3. Be intentional. Make sure they don't have every gadget that all their friends have. If they grow up not having all these things, they will be less likely to demand them. Don't automatically provide them with everything they desire. Just because you can afford something doesn't mean you should buy it for them. Hang this verse from Philippians 4 on the door of their bedrooms:

> I know what it is to be in need, and I know what it is to have plenty. I have learned the secret of being content in any and every situation, whether well fed or hungry, whether living in plenty or in want. (v. 12)

4. Throughout the year, expose them to those less fortunate than themselves. Make sure they participate in mission trips to third-world countries, do work projects in poorer parts of your city or state, or regularly, as a family, work in soup kitchens or other ministries to feed the homeless.

5. Make sure they get a job as soon as they are old enough. Allowances stop at this point, and they learn to manage the money they make from working. One of the best ways to avoid developing feelings of entitlement is learning to work. Let me say that again—learning to work is the greatest attitude adjuster ever.

9

Rethinking Social Media
and Smartphone Use

> *One set of parents told me in my office that they finally
> had to tell their fifteen-year-old son that he must place his
> phone on the kitchen counter each night by 10 p.m. so that
> he would stop abusing it by constantly texting until the wee
> hours of the morning. They were expecting substantial push
> back to this new requirement and were surprised and quite
> proud that he agreed to comply and immediately did as he
> was asked. They were shocked, however, the next morning
> when they came downstairs for their morning coffee to find
> him curled up sound asleep on top of the kitchen counter
> with his cell phone cradled in his hand. When they woke
> him, helped him down from the counter, and demanded
> an explanation, all he could say was, "You guys just don't
> understand."*

Parents are always the last ones to the technology party. We
provide our kids with a plethora of electronic devices—

smartphones, gaming consoles, laptop computers, handheld tablets—and are completely caught off guard by the negative behaviors that result. I guess, when you think about it, there was a day when parents were stunned to find out their kids had the audacity to make their own fire in the back of the cave or to stay up late at night talking on the newfangled telephone, even though only two other people in the entire town had one. Or there was my mom, who repeatedly had to tell me to go to bed and stop playing Pong. Google it. It was magic.

Modern technology has been thrust on us, and we are all scrambling to find out its benefits and its dangers. Most families have struggled to come up with a coherent strategy regarding how exactly to integrate this technology into their lives. Strategies have ranged from total prohibition to "anything goes" to something akin to outright confusion. So let's try to clear up some of the confusion by spending the next few pages formulating a comprehensive strategy for social media and smartphone use and their role in our families' lives. First, let's examine a few reasons this strategy is so important.

Social Media Enmeshment

You may remember I mentioned the amazing speaker and author, Simon Sinek, in chapter 8. Well, in that same interview, he had this to say about young people and social media:

> We know that engagement with social media and our cell phones releases a chemical called dopamine. That's why when

you get a text, it feels good. That's why we count the "likes," and if our Instagram is going slower, we think, "Did I do something wrong? Do they not like me anymore?" It's why it is traumatic for young kids to be "unfriended." Because we know that when you get it (that social media response), you get a hit of dopamine. Which feels good, and that's why we keep going back to it. Dopamine is the exact same chemical that is released when we smoke, drink, and gamble. In other words, it is highly, highly addictive.

We have age restrictions on smoking, drinking, and gambling, and no age restrictions on social media and cell phones. You have an entire generation that has access to an addictive, numbing chemical called dopamine, through social media and cell phones, as they are going through the high stress of adolescence. Now, because we are allowing unfettered access to these dopamine-producing devices, it's becoming hardwired, so as they grow older, so many kids don't know how to form deep meaningful relationships . . . their words, not mine. The science is clear. We know that people who spend more time on Facebook suffer higher rates of depression than those that spend less time on Facebook.[1]

What is the first thing our kids engage with in the morning? What is the one item that has become the most indispensable thing our children use throughout the day? What is the last thing our kids' eyes focus on right before they fall asleep? If you answered their smartphone, you would be correct. That little electronic marvel has become an ever-present fixation in their lives. It is the epicenter around which all else revolves. A recent study showed that 50 percent of teens say they are addicted to their smartphones. In fact, 72 percent stated they are compelled to answer all texts immediately, and 78 percent said they check their phones at least hourly.[2] This same Pew Research study also found that one in four teenagers are online "almost constantly," and another large portion are on their smartphones a good part of the day.[3]

A recent survey conducted among conservative parents of children under the age of eighteen by the American Culture & Faith Institute revealed that parents are well aware of the dangers of too much social media engagement by their kids. Almost nine out of ten of those parents (86 percent) said their children are worse off for their exposure to social media exchanges. Further, six out of ten of those parents (61 percent) said smartphones subtract value from their kids' lives.[4] Yet we continue to allow our kids to own these devices. Nielsen reported that smartphone ownership among teenagers was 36 percent in 2001 and had nearly doubled to 70 percent in 2013.[5] A 2015 national survey of teens by Common Sense Media found that the typical teen devotes about nine hours every day to media use and almost three hours each day to smartphone use alone.[6]

This is all new, by the way. And when I say new, I mean this is new to humans as a species. People have never been socially connected 24/7—ever. I'm sure this type of constant connection has its upside, but I see the negative impact in my office every day. Teens report feelings of depression when not on their phones, feelings of heightened anxiety when off their phones out of fear that they have missed out on something important, and sleep disturbance. They are also involved in numerous auto accidents due to texting while driving, and they attempt suicide more often when access to their smartphones is restricted.

When we can clearly see the many negatives associated with one particular activity, it doesn't take a genius to figure out that we have a problem in our hands—or pockets or purses, wherever you happen to keep it. It seems evident that we, as human beings, are not created for constant social connection. John Donne was famous for saying, "No man is an island," but we're learning that no man is Grand Central Station either.

The Falsification of Relationships

Nathan was a sixteen-year-old boy whose parents brought him to my office for counseling because they were concerned about his constant gaming and social isolation, as well as a demeanor that had them afraid he might be depressed. During the intake assessment, I asked him about his social group.

> Me: *So, Nathan, would you say you have few friends or lots of friends?*
>
> Nathan: *Oh, I have a bunch of friends.*
>
> Me: *How many close friends? They know everything about you and you know everything about them?*
>
> Nathan: *I guess I have three really close friends.*
>
> Me: *So are these school friends? Neighborhood friends? Church friends?*
>
> Nathan: *Nope, they're in my clan. You know, WOW? Dude, World of Warcraft.*
>
> Me: *Oh, sorry. So where do these guys live?*
>
> Nathan: *Let's see. Jonathan lives in New York, Donis is in Dallas, and Trey lives in some little town in Puerto Rico.*

So Nathan had never met in person those he considered his closest friends in the world. This is one aspect of *Online Friendship Falsification*, which refers to online "friendships" being regarded as authentic. These types of "friendships" are relationships of a sort, but they are not to be confused with real-life, authentic friendships. Kids like Nathan truly feel as though online friends are the real deal—solid friends with whom they are connected on multiple levels. I see kids all the time who brag about the fact that they have more than two thousand friends on Facebook or one thousand followers on Instagram. They seem to believe that these people are actually friends who are close to them. I had another thirteen-year-old female client who had inappropriate contact with a forty-year-old pedophile she believed was another thirteen-year-old "friend" on Facebook.

Today's teens have a compulsive need to be "liked" on social media, a sprinkle of fame gained from having a large number of friends. Many kids measure their self-worth based on these indicators, as though the limelight were the only light worth pursuing. And this nonstop need to be "liked" has taken peer pressure to a whole new level. We have all experienced peer pressure at some point in our lives. It's a common experience that is a rite of passage during one's younger years; however, that pressure has been ramped up through the power of social media. Kids now feel compelled to post pics of the latest party they went to, who they were with, what they did, what they ate, and what they wore. They wonder, *Do I appear as happy as my friends? Am I having as much fun as my friends? Do I look as good as my friends? Is my house as nice as the houses my friends live in?* This is twenty-four hours a day, seven days a week of constant social comparison. And these comparisons come with immediate feedback in the form of "likes," "hearts," "hugs," approving emojis, disapproving emojis, and on and on. There are also the status boosts affiliated with adopting the moniker BFF (Best Friends Forever) or your boyfriend making your relationship FO (Facebook Official).

In addition to peer pressure, bullying has achieved even greater heights of ease and effectiveness. Kids can now be called fat, ugly, loser, slut, weirdo, or a worthless piece of %^#@ not only at school, to be laughed at by all their peers, but also online by an invisible body of peers from around the world. They are now subject to bullying that lasts all day and night, every day and night, from a global network of friends, foes, fools, and frauds. No child is safe—not even in the security of their own home or bedroom—from having their heart shredded, their worldview mocked, their reputation destroyed, and their soul tormented.

The Falsification of Communication

Stewart was a sophomore in college and came into my office very depressed and downtrodden. He informed me that he had broken up with his girlfriend of two years. They had gotten so serious that they had even considered marriage, so I was quite concerned with this news. When I asked him what had happened, he said she just didn't see their paths heading in the same direction; they had dreams that were too far apart. He told her he didn't agree but was not going to stand in her way if this is what she really wanted. I told him I was pleased that they were able to talk it out and that

> *things seemed settled for them to move on. When I asked*
> *him if he remembered anything else about the conversa-*
> *tion, he paused, reached into his pocket, and said, "I don't*
> *know. Let me look." After a two-year exclusive relationship,*
> *including the discussion of marriage, this long-term loving*
> *relationship was ended in a series of text messages. All I*
> *could think was, OMG!*

Good communication is so much more than 140 characters can express, and I don't care how many emojis you use; they cannot replace talking face-to-face. We, as a society, are losing the art of verbal communication. Texting is wonderful for casually keeping up with friends and family and relaying quick bits of information, but for hard, meaningful, relationship-building conversations, it is woefully inadequate. Albert Mehrabian's famous study found that a whopping 93 percent of our communication is nonverbal.[7] The vast majority of what we're trying to say is communicated through tone, facial expression, vocal inflection, and subtleties of eye contact. Online textual communication simply is not capable of doing the job that humans need it to do. What is lost when that nonverbal communication is missing? Many vital things, such as intent, motive, desire, empathy, emphasis, and true meaning, just to name a few.

Good verbal communication is an art form garnered over years of observation and practice throughout our early years. The current overreliance on textual communication is hampering this generation from acquiring this skill. Who knows how the relationship between Stewart and his girlfriend could have ended up if they would have spoken face-to-face?

The Falsification of Awareness

Numerous times I've had teens in my office who seemed wholly incapable of putting their phones down. It was in their hand, on their lap, or balanced on their knee, but wherever it was, it was within glancing distance. Lord knows they couldn't miss a single message. One young lady, right in the middle of what I felt was an extraordinary example of psychotherapeutic brilliance on my part, stopped looking at me and began reading what was on her phone. Many kids do this, so it didn't disturb me too much, but then she grinned to herself and began typing into her phone for a good minute or so. She finally noticed that I was still in the room and said, "Oh, sorry. My bad. Chrissy was about to buy the most unbelievably rancid outfit at Nordstrom. I had to put a stop to it. What would that girl do without me?"

Most of us have felt that urgency, that twinge of excitement, when we first open Facebook or Instagram. What's new? Have I missed anything important? Did I miss out on seeing the latest cute dog curled up on a comfy couch? This little adrenaline rush is known in cyber circles as ICYMI, or In Case You Missed It. What we adults feel as a slight rush of expectancy our kids feel as a full-on panic attack if they are not up to the nanosecond on the absolute latest peer news, pics, and gossip.

I've also noticed that when I'm at a ball game, concert, speaking event, or even church, many younger people are more concerned with shooting pics or vids and posting what they are experiencing than actually experiencing the moment. They can't get through an event without becoming consumed with how they are going to make their presence at the event go viral. I just want to gently, yet forcibly, remove the phone from their hand, hug them close, and assure them that it's going to be okay. "Shhh, it's okay. You are okay. You don't have to be plugged in every second of every day." Trust me, life and relationships don't need constant monitoring. In fact, life and relationships work much better when they are not monitored around the clock. Our souls, our emotions, our brains, our bodies need space—space to simply be, without the constant drone of the mundane that we have convinced ourselves is paramount. It's going to be interesting to see the long-term impact of a generation that has received no emotional or cognitive solitude. In all other aspects of the human experience, constant stimulation is never a good thing.

The Online Disinhibition Effect

> I actually knew Bryce in my personal life. Not well, but I knew he was a leader in the youth group at our church. As a senior, he filled in to speak to the youth group on occasion and planned to attend Bible college and become a minister. His parents were noticeably flustered when they sat down to talk to me. They told me that recent events had left them quite perplexed. They had never monitored Bryce's social media or smartphone use because he had never been in trouble and they just didn't see the need to. Then one day his mother found his laptop open in his room as she was putting away some of his clean clothes. Just on a whim, she decided to see what he was up to online. Well, the computer was open to Facebook, and she was instantly appalled by what she saw. There were photos that bordered on lewd, and all his language was drenched in profanity, with vulgar references to sex, drugs, and alcohol use. His dad exclaimed, "Our son is Dr. Jekyll and Mr. Hyde! He's one person in real life and some total deviant

> *online. We are his parents, and we have no earthly idea who this kid really is!"*

This scenario is quite common for many parents. Many find that their kids seem to display different personalities when communicating with friends online. It can be jolting to find out their little Sunday-school attender morphs into some profane reprobate online. This phenomenon actually has a name. It's called the *Online Disinhibition Effect*. This is when someone, while online, loses all their social or moral restraints that are normally present while interacting with people face-to-face. Someone who is a nice, modest, Christian young lady while with her family turns into a sexually suggestive, pot-advocating party animal while online.

This "effect" is the result of many things, including the anonymity that online communication provides. Typing on a screen gives people the impression that "no one knows who I really am." Communicating online also allows a person to *project* a persona that may be a far cry from their normal personality. It allows kids to put on masks far easier than in real life and to say and claim things they never would while communicating face-to-face. And many kids feel that since it's all happening online, in cyberspace, it's not real and not to be taken seriously. "I just talk like that with my friends online. It's no biggie, jeez," they say.

One of the most obvious and notorious versions of the Online Disinhibition Effect is trolling. Trolling is when someone interacts on social media by instigating arguments with the intent to agitate and cause trouble. Trolls post incendiary, irrelevant comments for the sole purpose of provoking a negative emotional response, simply because they think it would be funny. Many kids love to share stories at school of their trolling exploits in an attempt at achieving social recognition.

And if you thought the Online Disinhibition Effect was some impressive psychobabble, how about *Solipsistic Introjections*. No, I did not just make up that term. This phenomenon occurs when we get the sense that our minds have merged with another person or persons online, and an alternative reality is created. You heard me right, an alternative reality—as in nice kids acting like they're members of a biker gang online.

Electronic Seclusion

A common complaint I hear from parents who come to see me in my office is that they never see their child. "They walk in the door from school and head straight to their room," they confess. "They come out, wolf down some food, and then head straight back into their room for the rest of the evening! I feel like our family is broken." I would have to agree with these parents—our families are sort of broken. The ironic thing is that we, the parents, keep buying the hammer.

Many of us lament the fact that our families don't talk anymore or never spend quality time together anymore. But when birthdays come around, what do we buy our children? You guessed it, the latest smartphone, gaming system, tablet, or laptop. We keep providing the very instruments that lead to this family fragmentation. As mentioned in a previous chapter, in our zeal to keep up with our secular culture's emphasis on materialism, we feel compelled to make sure our kids are not the slightest bit different from their peers by providing them with every electronic gadget conceived by humankind. So the actual source of this division or broken-ness in our families can be traced to us or, more precisely, our wallets.

What's more is that our self-inflicted technology not only physically separates family members within the home but also can keep us completely isolated while we are all in the same room. How many times have you been in your living room with several family members, yet there is virtually no dialogue between you? You could all reach out and touch one another, but you are myopically focused on the smartphones in your hands. A crazy uncle could prance naked through the room and not one person would notice, which, of course, might be a really good thing.

Family Sabbath Rest

Finally, let's talk about some solutions. When God said in Exo-dus 23:12, "Six days thou shalt do thy work, and on the seventh day thou shalt rest" (KJV), He was not casually suggesting something. It was a command from the Lord God Almighty. Yet we live in a society that has quite literally removed God from the Christian's Sabbath day. Today families have soccer games, gymnastics tournaments, baseball games, a myriad of social events, school activities, and every shopping opportunity imaginable on the Sabbath. Families are run ragged on Sundays, just like they were any other day on their hectic family calendar. But rest is essential. It was even essential for God to rest after the sixth day of creation. He *chose* to rest! For some reason, we cannot be bothered or delayed by the notion. Today's culture is running at breakneck speed, 24/7, to have it all, do it all, get credit for it all, and post those accomplishments online.

As believers, we don't have to follow the world's ruinous example. In fact, Paul instructs us in 2 Corinthians 6:17, "Therefore, 'Come out from them and be separate, says the Lord. Touch no unclean thing, and I will receive you.'" God calls us to separate ourselves from our secular culture, not in love or service but in rejection of sinful practices, such as making God's holy Sabbath just another day in the rat race. In fact, in Exodus 31:16, God tells us that keeping the Sabbath will be a sign between Him and us throughout all generations. Well, those of us called by His Name in *this* generation are leaving God and His promised sign hanging unobserved.

So, children of God, let's honor and please our heavenly Father, shall we? I feel it is imperative as we move forward through this bleary-eyed, chronically fatigued culture that we slam on the brakes for the sake of our families' sanity and spirit. And let me set your mind at ease. This family Sabbath rest is not all that difficult to organize or pull off. It is actually quite simple and easy. When you look at the big picture, it consists of only four things:

1. *Abstain from any outside family activity that is not Christ-related.* This means no sports, school events, social organizations, work, or social engagements that separate the family.

2. *Abstain from any electronic activity that separates the family.* This includes video games (unless the whole family is playing), phones, TV (unless the family is watching it together), laptops, iPads, etc.

3. *Turn all phones completely off.* Do whatever it takes to make this happen. If necessary, take out the batteries

and lock them in the family safe, but make it happen. (It's reasonable to leave one of the parents' phones accessible for essential communication only.)

4. *Every couple of months, skip church and go do an all-day activity with your family.* I know this is going to get me in hot water, but . . . there . . . I said it, and no lightning bolt has struck me yet. Have a family worship time, then go hang out together.

Now, this is not going to be easy because it will require you to make some hard choices. If you choose to establish a family Sabbath rest, you and your kids will not be participating in activities that *everybody else* is doing. But what a great opportunity! Remember when Joshua said, "But if serving the Lord seems undesirable to you, then choose for yourselves this day whom you will serve, whether the gods your ancestors served beyond the Euphrates, or the gods of the Amorites, in whose land you are living. But as for me and my household, we will serve the Lord" (Josh. 24:15)? This is very much a Joshua moment for you and your family. When that select baseball coach tells you your ten-year-old is destined for the majors if only you'll pay three thousand dollars for him to play games every weekend, including Sundays, you will have the opportunity *with your kids by your side* to "choose for yourselves this day whom you will serve." When you turn down that coach and see the bewilderment on his face, you will understand the profound impact this stand will have on your child. Simply unplugging for one day each week encourages familial, spiritual, emotional, physical, and relational health and wellness.

Ten New Electronic Commandments

Okay, to practically address the issues described in this chapter and promote a more unified and cohesive family, I now suggest these ten new electronic commandments for the home. Granted, it would be much more dramatic if these were etched on stone tablets, but ink on a page will simply have to do.

#1 *Parents Set the Standard*

No change can be made in how electronics are utilized in the home if the parents do not set the standard. Mom and Dad, if we want our kids to be more engaged with the family, more focused on family than on "likes" and "comments," then we have to set the pace by being more focused on the family ourselves. If we don't reduce our own fixation with our phones, then our kids don't stand a chance.

#2 *Regulate, Don't Prohibit*

Simply acting as though this technology doesn't exist is not the answer. Denying our age-appropriate children smartphones is also not the answer. At some point, they must learn how to use them properly. However, when we do provide this technology to our kids, we must monitor and regulate their usage of it. Regulations such as no phones once they get home from school—I'm not kidding—no phones at the dinner table, no phones allowed in a restaurant during a family meal, and no phones after a certain time are a must.

#3 *No Smartphones until Age Sixteen*

Thirteen-year-olds don't vote, drive, or join the armed services for a reason. Tweens and young teens don't have the cognitive wherewithal to make good decisions. They have way too many synapses that are not connected yet. If they cannot be trusted to drive a car until they are sixteen, then they should not be trusted to use a smartphone. Everything we want our kids to have a phone for is accomplished in the "dumb" part of the phone (texting and calling), and everything they get in trouble for (sexting, porn, social media overuse) is accomplished in the "smart" part of the phone. So when a twelve-year-old is caught sexting with a classmate, that's not a smartphone problem; that's a dumb-parent problem for giving them access to technology in the first place.

#4 *Unequivocal Understanding as to the Ownership of Any Electronic Device*

The phone does not belong to the child. Repeat this with me: *the phone does not belong to the child.* It belongs to the parent who purchased the phone for the child; therefore, that parent has the absolute right to view what's on that phone at any point, at any time.

#5 *No Passwords and 24/7 Parental Access*

In keeping with the spirit of commandment #4, there should be no use of passwords on any device. I would include parents, unless their job requires confidential communication. This allows the parent to randomly verify what's on the child's phone at any point they see fit. And if your child wants to look at your phone . . . tell them to be your guest.

#6 *Parents Control Apps*

Your child can download apps whose sole intent is to hide other apps on the phone that you would disapprove of. I mention this because we fight a losing battle trying to keep up with all the apps our kids are constantly downloading onto their phones, and some of these apps are extremely harmful for underage kids. That is why it's important to talk with your phone provider and make sure no app can be downloaded to your child's phone without your knowledge and permission. A great resource for parents in this regard is www.iparent.tv. This website teaches parents all they need to know about the apps on their kids' phones, including whether they are acceptable or dangerous.

#7 *All Electronic Usage Has a Set End Time Each Night*

You've heard it said that "a watched pot never boils." Well, a child left with their smartphone in bed unregulated never sleeps. Set a nightly curfew for when all electronics need to be shut off. This can be done without too much of an altercation by simply setting a time limit on their phone with your phone provider. For example, at 10 p.m., the phone simply stops working.

#8 *All Devices with Internet Access Have Blocking Software*

This one is an absolute no-brainer, yet I'm stunned by the number of parents who hand their adolescent child a smartphone with full access to all the internet has to offer. That's the equivalent of getting them a pet rattlesnake, then being surprised when they get bit. I don't have the space to expound on all the mind-numbing dangers that lurk on the internet, so just trust me when I say that all internet-capable devices should be safeguarded with blocking software.

#9 *Time Limits for Video Gaming*

There is no longer any debate that video gaming is addictive. Unlimited access to gaming can be harmful to your child academically, socially, emotionally, and, in many cases, morally and spiritually. Therefore, make sure your child's participation is not unlimited. You determine the number of hours per week that you're comfortable with, then it's off the computer and into the backyard to play badminton—or something.

#10 *Age-Appropriate Video Games Only*

A kid told me the other day, "Most of these games are kind of like R-rated movies. Lots of violence, blood, profanity, and a few topless girls." No matter how popular a particular game may be, if you don't permit your eleven-year-old to attend R-rated movies—and, in case you're wondering, you shouldn't—then the same should apply to these games.

The technology we have at our disposal is crazy when you think about it. My father was born in a horse-drawn wagon on a cattle ranch, yet I have a device in my pocket that allows me to FaceTime a friend in South Africa. It is wonderful in so many respects. It does, however, bring with it some drawbacks and pitfalls for our families. Regulation and monitoring is the answer, not all-out prohibition. Again, we should be preparing our children to utilize this technology appropriately when they leave our homes, and that takes planning and purpose in regard to how and when we allow them to surf the web, use advanced software applications, and utilize communications capabilities.

Five Practical Changes You Can Make Today

1. Take a cold, hard look at *your* smartphone and computer use. Are you perusing Facebook during dinner or poring over Twitter for the umpteenth time while the entire family is in the room? We, as parents, can't hope to get the speck out of the eyes of our children if we don't address the giant redwood in our own.

2. Call a family meeting to address changes in how you are going to be utilizing smartphones and social media moving forward. Have these new guidelines written down to avoid any ambiguity.

3. Contact your phone provider for information on how to set time limits on your child's phone and how to make all apps flow through your parental control.

4. If your child already has a smartphone loaded with apps, find out how to wipe it clean so that you and your child can together decide which apps are appropriate moving forward.

5. Implement the ten new electronic commandments ASAP.

10

The Porn-Again Child

When I tell you that sixteen-year-old Eric was a good kid, you have to believe me—he was a good kid. The entire family was smart and successful. They were all, in some way or another, involved in ministry inside and outside their local church, and Eric, his parents agreed, led the way. He was also captain of the soccer team and a leader in Young Life. This is why they were so stunned one day when Eric's twin sister ran into their bedroom to tell them what had just happened. She frantically told them that she couldn't find her iPad, so she decided to borrow Eric's, since he was still at soccer practice. When she opened the tablet, she was stunned to find an open video of herself, naked in the shower! She was even more astounded to find five other "voyeur videos" of herself in varying degrees of undress. Eric's parents soon learned that he had been regularly viewing hardcore pornography since the age of ten. When they confronted him as to why he took the videos of his sister, he

> *very remorsefully admitted to showing them to his soccer buddies, then selling them to a porn site for extra money.*

We have a generation of young people who literally have been raised on pornography. And the available sources of porn grow every day. It's no longer enough to make sure our kids' desktop computers have a filter; they can now access porn from their laptops, tablets, Xboxes, PlayStations, iPads, and, most important, smartphones. Pornography and its sexual perversion have taught kids from an early age what is sexually exciting, sensual, and erotic. That creates a sad truth. The spouses they will eventually marry will not have a snowball's chance in Hades of living up to the sexual expectations established by thousands of hardcore porn videos.

Remember those innocent days of yesteryear, when we were all so upset about sex being taught in the local high schools? How quaint. Now we have to worry about what our children are learning about group sex, gay and lesbian sex, bondage, sadomasochism, bestiality, urination, defecation, and simulated rape online long before they hit junior high!

A Sex-Saturated Culture

This chapter is not simply about pornography on the internet; it's about HBO, Pay-per-view, sexting, the *Sports Illustrated Swimsuit Issue*, roadside billboards for strip clubs (euphemistically renamed "gentlemen's clubs"), kids at school with clothing that barely covers their private areas, the expectation of sexual activity (early and often), and every young person's sexual exploits being videoed and shared with friends online. One young lady told me that "tons" of girls at her junior high school had been solicited for a nude selfie, and one fourteen-year-old boy said that looking at nude pics of girls in his school is what "you guys used to call flirting."

The reality is that pornography has become a way of life for many teenagers in our country. It is rare these days for a teenager not to be exposed to porn at some point during adolescence. A recent Barna Group study among twelve- to seventeen-year-olds found that three out of every ten say they look at porn every week; half view it at least once a month; and only one out of every five say they never access porn. It is so commonplace among them that only one out of every three teens believes it is always or usually wrong—immoral, in adult parlance—to view pornographic images. To show how distorted their sense of morality is becoming, the study found that teens are nearly twice as likely to consider the failure to recycle and 50 percent more likely to label overeating to be immoral as to portray porn in the same manner.[1]

Even fewer—just one out of four—feel it is wrong to watch sexually explicit scenes in TV shows or movies. That helps explain why 85 percent of them frequently seek out or watch videos of pornographic activity. The days of flipping the pages of *Playboy* magazine and getting ahold of X-rated videos or DVDs is a thing of the past. Everything they want is now available in real time on their smartphones, tablets, or computers—for free.[2]

When teens talk to one another about porn—which they do more often than you'd like—nine out of ten of them do so in an encouraging, accepting, or neutral way. Not many of them experience feelings of guilt regarding porn use. That mentality helps explain why a majority of teens have sent or received sexts from peers—about two-thirds have sent and nearly half have received sext messages.[3]

In case you're wondering, the research shows that Christian teens are just as likely to engage with pornography as their peers, although they are more likely to feel guilty about it. That's the good news—at least they know it is wrong. The Barna study found that 70 percent of church youth pastors have had teens approach them for help with a porn problem in the past year. Most of those kids were boys—perhaps because most youth pastors are guys—but there are substantial numbers of Christian girls who have also sought such help from a youth leader. Pornography use is a widespread and growing problem—one that is not even seen as a problem by our young people.[4]

This chapter is about a sex-saturated culture that we can't keep our kids away from, even if we shipped them to the North Pole until college. Sex is unavoidable, ubiquitous, inescapable—you pick the adjective. We've already discussed blocking software in this book, so we're not going to be discussing that again. This chapter is about how to raise Jesus-loving kids who will shine like stars in the midst of a perverse generation.

The Long-Term Impact of a Sex-Saturated Culture

Objectification of Women

A sixteen-year-old boy sat in my office recently and was telling me about his new girlfriend. When he took out his phone to show me her picture, he said, "Dude, check it out.

This is what I f@$% every weekend!" Notice that he didn't say, "This is *who* I f@$%." He used the word *what*. Using the word *what* denotes an object or thing, as opposed to a human being.

This young man's attitude is the perfect example of the *objectification of women*. He doesn't consider his girlfriend a person; she is a beautiful "thing" that he can use for his own sexual enjoyment. When a guy views many sexually suggestive images involving women, he begins seeing them as a collection of body parts, not as human beings. In fact, porn is actually broken down into categories that focus on specific details, such as large breasts, big backsides, long legs, blonde hair, certain ethnicities, age—it's like picking out a car with a sunroof or other precise features you desire. This fixation on body parts or types of bodies can then morph into fetishes in which a guy can actually have a sexual experience by doing nothing more than looking at a woman's foot. A foot! This overexposure to sexually explicit material turns all women from the people God created them to be into a collection of body parts to be used for a man's sexual gratification.

To take the point even further, I will share the story of a middle-aged stockbroker with a porn addiction who was recently in my office and told me he had fallen off the wagon and was feeling very regretful about it. As I have done with previous addicts, I asked him to close his eyes and recount the last pornographic scene he had seen. I instructed him to be as graphically accurate as possible. Who was there? He told me five men and one young girl. At my insistence, he described where they were, what they were doing, what it sounded like, and what music was playing. Then I asked him to imagine that young lady in the scene and replace her with his fifteen-year-old daughter. His eyes shot open. He looked at me with disgust on his face and said, "That's just sick!"

Yes. Yes, it is. It's sick no matter who the young lady is. So it seems sexual perversion is exciting when the woman is an object, but it's "sick" when the woman is an actual person.

Pornographic Progression

The first time a kid has a taste of beer, they probably feel a little woozy after just a few swigs. It takes a little more after they've been drinking for a few years, and should they become an alcoholic later in life, it might take a couple of six packs before they feel that same wooziness. The same desensitization occurs with sexual addiction. When it comes to sex, it's all about the buzz. When a kid first sees a picture of a naked person, they experience a surge of excitement! Wow! It's so exciting, so titillating, so wrong! That's the buzz. The buzz comes from seeing or doing something that is taboo or forbidden. And when a kid goes from still photos to moving pornographic videos? The buzz is electrifying!

The *Pornographic Progression* is all about chasing that buzz. So after a kid sees hundreds of videos showing a man and a woman having sex, it loses, you guessed it, the buzz. Been there, done that. Therefore, what do they have to do? That's right—find something *more* taboo, *more* forbidden to generate the desired level of buzz. Soon the kid is introduced to fetishes, as they turn to videos of more unconventional sexual activities. As you can imagine, after years of this type of escalation, there are very few sexual perversions they have not viewed. And when a kid has seen it all, there comes a time when the buzz cannot be achieved with any video. Just sitting and watching will no longer cut it. As they continue to chase the buzz, the next step is to have an in vivo experience—to live out these sexual fantasies. Because the Pornographic Progression starts so early, kids are engaging in their first real-life sexual experience at a younger and younger age.

This sexual activity is being demonstrated in varying ways in today's adolescent culture. Several years ago, it wasn't considered a really good college party until a bunch of girls started making out with one another. Where do you think that expectation came from? Websites will give college students tens of thousands of dollars to film group sex in their dorms, and these videos are being watched by hundreds of thousands of people, including numerous prepubescent boys. So an outbreak of raunchy sexual activity at parties is now expected at many junior high get-togethers. And in the quest for the next perverted buzz, homosexuality is often included. In fact, it's thought that more than 20 percent of homosexual porn is being viewed by heterosexual men.[5] What could be more taboo or forbidden, and therefore take them to the next level, than homosexuality?

This normalizing of homosexual sexual activity shows itself in the ever-increasing embrace of bisexuality by young women and men; by homosexual sex acts becoming more normative in college fraternity and sorority initiation rites; and by boys and girls as young as sixth grade finding it socially beneficial to proudly proclaim themselves to be bisexual, lesbian, gay, polysexual, pansexual, or transsexual. Now, the vast majority of these young people are not these things, but if they can be perceived as being cutting edge, unbound by social norms, it will garner them additional "likes" on Facebook. Mission accomplished.

By the way, that a majority of people under age thirty now deem bisexual and homosexual living choices to be moral and reasonable is more a reflection of a worldview gone bad than a newly adopted lifestyle. Roughly 4 percent of the adult population is currently homosexual or bisexual. That figure is higher among teens and college students but remains a very small minority of the population. Still, the trend is not encouraging.

Early Onset Sexual Dysfunction

It used to be that erectile dysfunction was reserved for elderly men whose hormones were just about ready to give up the ghost. However, I recently met with a young man who was a sophomore at an Ivy League school who told me that when he would try to have sex with his girlfriend, he could not maintain an erection. The only way he could have even nominal success was to concentrate really hard on a particularly arousing porn video while attempting intercourse with the young woman. Oh, and just a few weeks ago, a sexually active fifteen-year-old young man told me the same thing. "Dude, I can't keep it up any more without, you know, focusing on porn." Seems crazy, right?

But you see, porn is the perfect sexual experience. Every time you view it, you get exactly what you desire. You get the precise woman you want—the right hair color, the right age, the right build. And this perfect woman performs the exact sexual activities you love the most, and you are sexually satisfied every single time. There is, obviously, one major drawback to this perfect sexual experience . . . you're alone. Not only is the perfect woman not present, but also no woman is present. This entire rapturous experience is taking place in one person's head. So when a young man moves from years of "perfect" sexual encounters to a real sexual encounter, with a real-life woman, he finds out that sex isn't perfect. It involves another person—a person with feelings, desires, a spirit, and sometimes a fragile self-image. What these kids (and millions of adults, for that matter) don't understand is that sex is a beautiful, God-given, outward expression of the love God has given to two people. It's intimate and giving, not raunchy and all about getting your own sexual needs met. This porn-to-person sexual transition is very difficult for many young men to make.

A Proactive Approach to the Problem

Okay, let me begin by saying that many of you are going to be slightly uncomfortable with some of the suggestions that will follow. However, please keep in mind that how we, as parents, have handled the issue of sexuality in our homes up to this point has not been very successful. By the time teens leave high school, about half of them have had sexual intercourse with one or more opposite-sex partners. More than nine times out of ten, the sexual encounters our kids have are consensual and desired. Among the kids who do not have sexual intercourse before they graduate, the most common reason for abstaining is because it conflicts with their morals or religious beliefs. Unfortunately, only one-third of the young virgins give that answer. In fact, past research has shown that the rates of sexual activity among Christian adolescents and non-Christian adolescents are statistically indistinguishable, so let's be open to addressing this issue in a different way moving forward.[6]

Many of us grew up in families that tended to ignore the subject of sex altogether, unless events made the discussion necessary. For example, I was walking home from school in the fourth grade with my best friend, when he told me that people "f@#$" to have a baby. I don't know how, but I had some vague understanding as to what that word meant and I was utterly disgusted. So I proceeded to tell him that this was totally incorrect. I told him in no uncertain terms that when two people love each other, the proof that they love each other is that a baby comes out. Who doesn't know this? I couldn't understand how he could concoct such a gross idea. "Nope," he said, "people f@#$ to have babies." Well, when I got home, I marched in the back door and promptly asked my mother, who was washing dishes at the sink, "Mom, do people 'f@#$' to have babies?" The look on my sweet mother's face clearly suggested that a discussion of sex had now become necessary.

Unfortunately, many of us don't handle addressing the topic with our kids very well. If we don't completely ignore it, we demonize it, effectively suggesting that anything associated with sexuality is dirty, disgusting, forbidden, sinful, filthy, and sordid. If a sexual word is uttered on television, or some song suggests something salacious on the radio, we lunge to turn the channel, with a deliberate muttering of how horrible it is that such a thing could possibly be broadcast. We tell our kids as they grow up that any personal sexual exploration is wrong and totally forbidden. And if they ever do explore their own sexuality, they will go blind, hair will grow on their palms, and the Lord God Almighty will judge them. "And you wouldn't want that, would you?" we say.

Where did we get this impression of sex? Certainly not from God or His Word. God loves sex. Did you read that? He loves it! He thinks it's the greatest, because He thought of it! It was His idea. In fact, one of the very first things He told us to do was "be fruitful and multiply" (Gen. 1:28 NLT). How do you think we were supposed to accomplish this command? Osmosis? And all you have to do is casually read through the Song of Solomon and you'll see quite clearly that God's purpose for sex is not simply procreation; it's for pleasure as well. Our heavenly Father's view of sex is so vastly different from what we are conveying to our children.

In fact, when we embrace the "sex is dirty" point of view, we are actually agreeing with this godless, porn-filled, sex-crazed culture. Our culture sees sex as being on the totally opposite end of the spectrum from the presence of God. This should not be our view. And not only is this a nonbiblical understanding of sex, but it also hasn't worked in keeping our kids sexually pure. Scaring them into abstinence has never worked. We follow Christ not out of fear of punishment but out of a strong desire to please the Father who loves us. So if scaring our kids into chastity isn't the answer, what is? Here are some practical steps we can take to lovingly, biblically, and intelligently prepare our kids in regard to sexuality.

Parents Needs to Educate Their Kids about Sex before the Internet and Culture Do

The most important step we can take in educating our kids about sex is to normalize it in our homes. We, as humans, tend to be afraid of or fascinated with things we are not familiar with or don't understand. Therefore, our goal should be to regard sex as a beautiful, meaningful, and natural aspect of a married couple's life. Let's stop pretending sex doesn't exist "in front of the children."

Now, if we begin to acknowledge the existence of this mythical marital practice openly in the home, what is bound to happen? That's right, we will all experience what my mom faced as she was doing the dishes that day; we will be forced to talk about it, explain it, and share God's Word about it. If you feel uneasy about assuming the role of sex-ed teacher for your kids, tons of Christian materials offer fun and easy ways for getting the information to them. How great would it be for our kids not to be shocked when other kids begin to discuss these matters at school? In fact, they can, at an early age, begin being used by God to clarify many of the misconceptions their friends are sharing.

And when we do talk with our kids about sex, or their genitals, we should be sure to use the actual clinical terms for body parts. To reference our "private parts" instead of using their actual names is to unknowingly denote shame. A vagina is a vagina, and a penis is a penis. There is nothing dirty about those words—or those body parts. My son, Josh, and his wife, Katie, have been working to reinforce this truth with their young family. One afternoon, not that long ago, Katie walked in on our three-year-old granddaughter, Ruthie, while she was sitting on the potty. She heard Ruthie singing out loud and clear, "Girls have 'ginas' and boys have 'peanuts.'" Well, it's a start.

Another aspect of acknowledging sexuality as a healthy human behavior is not to freak out at childhood sexual expression. Most kids at some point early in their lives will discover their "Oh my gosh, this feels great!" zone. One day they will reach between their legs and realize that their genitals have so many more nerve endings than most other parts of their body and that touching that area does feel really, really good. So when you find your child feeling their genitals or walk in on your adolescent son masturbating, do not overreact. Avoid getting agitated and saying things like, "Stop that! That's dirty!" or "What are you doing? You know that's nasty!" We should use this same approach when dealing with nudity. When a child is older and you find them walking around the house nude, refrain from lambasting them with a verbal onslaught about how disgusting their behavior is. Rather, simply use the episode to underscore the need for modesty. It is not appropriate to be nude when there are other people in the house. Instead of overreacting and saying things that instill shame in your child, use these times as teachable moments. Talk with and listen to your child, and try not to make these incidents big emotional events—for either of you.

Parents Need to Lead by Healthy Sexual Example

A child needs to see their mom and dad being romantic and affectionate with each other. They need to see Dad walk by and kiss Mom on the neck or Mom jump into Dad's lap and give him a big kiss on the lips. It's healthy for a child to notice their parents hugging and kissing! It shows them that their parents love each other and are physically/sexually attracted to each other. Why is this so important? Well, we want to take advantage of the opportunity to set the sexual expectations for our children. If our kids hit their preteen years having never seen healthy sexuality lived out before them, then we are leaving it to the porn industry and a depraved culture to set their sexual expectations.

Now, the next thing I'm going to suggest is going to be difficult for many of you. A child needs to know that their mommy and daddy have sex with each other. It's okay; take a deep breath and slowly exhale. It gets worse, because they need to know not only that their parents have sex but also that they love it, it's a blast, they can't wait to do it again, and it's a beautiful gift God has given to a husband and wife. Sex is not a hidden mystery; it's not some dirty, naughty activity that the older kids talk about and Mom and Dad keep locked away in secret. That approach creates a thrilling expectation in our kids. Remember, we want what we can't have and are fascinated with what is mysterious. Our goal for our children should be that they think sex is just a normal, regular thing they have known about forever—and that Mom and Dad say it is a wonderful part of being married.

One Important Related Note to Dad

Along this same line, it is vitally important that our sons see that their dads are sexually attracted to their mothers. I can't tell you how important this is. If they never see that Dad finds Mom sexually desirable, then we have left these boys to assume that the pretty models on TV or online are the only women worthy of being sexually desirable. This unconsciously encourages them to find porn and other sexually charged material enticing. You must, by example, show them that their mother is the hottest woman you have ever met, and those other women in the media hold no attraction to you. The thing that makes their mother sexy is not her physical appearance, but that she gave birth to them and has loved you through the good and bad times. And you have found her attractive since you were dating—and will continue to do so, even when you are both in your eighties. Our sons need to know that real women, like their moms, are worthy and deserving of our sexual desire and attraction.

Do we live in an oversexualized world? Yes. But that doesn't mean we have to simply roll over and accept it. Installing blocking software on all our kids' internet-accessible items is important, but it is not the only step we should take to combat the rampant hedonism. In fact, it's not even the most effective step. Normalizing sex in our homes by talking about it casually and often, as well as leading by example, are by far the most powerful weapons at a Christian parent's disposal so that our kids "may become blameless and pure, 'children of God without fault in a warped and crooked generation.' Then you will shine among them like stars in the sky" (Phil. 2:15).

Five Practical Changes You Can Make Today

1. First of all, if either you or your spouse has an issue with the compulsive use of pornography, it is critical that you seek help for the sake of your marriage and your kids. If you think it's not a problem and you can control your porn issue, remember that any aspect of your personal life that you keep secret is already out of control.

2. Begin the process of normalizing God's view of sex in your home. Acknowledge to your kid the existence of

sex in your marriage and begin to talk about it calmly and openly. Don't shut down sexual questions or discussions; encourage them and use them for His glory.

3. Purchase books and other resources to help you learn the best ways to discuss sexuality in an age-appropriate way with your kids. Their education in this matter is *your* job, not the school's or the church's job. It's your responsibility to make sure your kids are taught God's view of sex. Don't leave it up to the porn industry.

4. The health of your sex life is a reflection of the health of your marriage. So how healthy is your marriage? Never stop trying to make your sex life fun and exciting and a priority in your marriage. A failure in a couple's sex life is a major aspect of virtually every couple's breakup and divorce. Again, your greatest weapon to protect your kids against this sex-saturated culture is to model a healthy sex life. If your sexual relationship with your spouse is a problem, seek help from a counselor. It will be well worth it—not just for you and your spouse but for the ultimate good of your entire family.

5. Dad, begin to sexually, physically, and romantically show affection for your wife in front of your kids. Make PDA (public displays of affection) the norm in your home. Your kids may be grossed out at first, but they will love you for it later.

11

Parental Self-Worth and the Push

> *A father sat in front of me, desperate to explain to his wife and to me why he drives his son so hard in football. "Do I push my kid? Yeah. Guilty as charged. But my son is special! Everyone agrees with me that he has the physical, mental, and athletic ability to make it in the pros. Honey, don't you see that's why I personally train him an hour before his team practice starts and why I pay so much to have him work out with a personal position coach every Saturday. Expensive? Sure it is. But his future is worth it, isn't it? He is on track to be supersuccessful! You'll thank me for this one day, you'll see." The man's son was only nine years old.*

et's get something out of the way right up front. Brace yourselves. *Your child is not going to play professional sports.* Period. Not football, not baseball, not basketball, not soccer, not Tiddlywinks, not even jump rope. Your child will not participate in a single professional sport—nope, not one. And just a microscopic fraction of the nation's fifty-six million children will play college athletics. So to sum up, your child is going to play sports until they are about fourteen, or perhaps even in high school, and that's it.

Time for a statistical reality check. About fifty-six million school-age children, ages five through eighteen, are in the United States today. An astounding thirty-six million of them will play some level of sports, either on school teams or on teams organized outside of school. This year roughly three million teens, covering their freshman through senior years, will play on one or more high school teams. If we jump ahead to see how many of those high school athletes will eventually make it to the professional level in their chosen sport—whether it be a major sport, such as football or basketball, or a less high-profile sport, such as tennis or soccer—roughly only twelve hundred boys and girls from this year's graduating class will reach the professional level. To put that in statistical terms, that represents .04 percent of the year's senior class. That's less than 1 percent. In fact, it is less than one-tenth of 1 percent. Okay, it's exactly four one-hundredths of 1 percent. That's one out of every twenty-five hundred students. Your kid has a better chance of becoming a doctor, a millionaire, a military officer, a contestant on a TV reality show, or an elected official than becoming a professional athlete.[1]

So, parent, hear this: you and your youngster should enjoy your child's athletic career while you can, because they are not going to the pros. Invest your resources into helping them refine their mind, heart, and talent to master something else, because it's extremely unlikely that sports will be their best shot to rise to the top. Sure, that may be a big disappointment, but you need to get over it and begin to prepare them for a profession other than sports. Now that you have heard the heartbreaking truth, let that truth set you free. In the long run, you'll be glad you heeded our advice.

Perhaps you have not encountered it yet, but there is a thriving universe of superhyped, intense sports teams trolling for your kids. It's all part of America's overemphasized, win-at-all-costs youth sports machine. This insanity has produced a generation of children grasping for any reason for their teachers, coaches, parents, or even God to be proud of them. The "perform like an all-star or you're not worthy, because second place just means you're a loser" mentality is not toughening up our kids or making them more successful, but it *is* warping their view of themselves and the purpose God has for them in this life.

The Push

I remember back in elementary school how much I looked forward to Little League season every year. The uniforms, the cleats, the fans, the lights, the babes. It was such a special time of year that has been lost on this present generation. Today, for many families, there is nothing special about baseball season, because it comes right after soccer season, which immediately follows basketball season, which follows right after football season. Starting before they even begin school, kids are playing sports nonstop, all year round, filling their calendars with back-to-back practices and games. One eleven-year-old boy sat in my office and told me that when he got home at the end of the day, he would head straight into the shower and then go right to bed. I thought that was a weird after-school ritual, so I inquired further as to what time he actually got home from school and he told me about 9:00 or 9:30 every night. What?

I then inquired as to what took him so long to get home. He told me that right after school his family takes his sister to ballet, then it's off to his soccer practice. His brother waits in the car until that practice is over, then they pick up his sister and all go to drop off his brother at lacrosse practice. There they wait in the car, doing homework and eating a hearty, "healthy" meal from McDonald's or some similar fast-food nutrition haven until his brother is done, then they all finally head home. And that's just on Tuesdays and Thursdays. On Mondays and Wednesdays, his brother has select baseball practice, his sister has gymnastics, and he has lacrosse.

And so it goes, day after day, week after week of "the push." The push has families constantly coming and going, and throughout the entire year they have little or no time to simply stop—stop and sit in the backyard to watch the sunset, stop and sit in the living room to read a book, or stop and catch crawdads in the creek. Do kids even catch crawdads anymore? Do they even know what a crawdad is?

The first aspect of the push is that sports become a never-ending, vital part of a child's life. Every day of every season there are shin guards to put on and uniforms to wash. All kids have the pressure to perform at school, but these kids now have to perform in the classroom and on the field of play, nonstop throughout the year. That's a fun scenario for some, but a high-pressure, endless minefield of impossible expectations for others.

Year-Round Specialization

The push gets cranked up a notch when year-round sports get morphed into year-round specialization in only one sport.

Some eagle-eye dad has spotted pro-pitching talent in his six-year-old, so soccer or swimming bite the dust in the new race to hone the young Roger Clemens's hurling skills. This kid is now focused solely on refining his awesomeness in baseball. To be clear, this means his little arm, shoulder, and elbow are going to be performing the same repetitive movement thousands of times a year with no relief.

I asked a friend of mine once if he worried about his ten-year-old son damaging his arm by pitching a baseball all year round. He said, "Nope, not worried a bit. I ice his shoulder and elbow after every throwing session." Of course, my thought was, *Why is a ten-year-old doing anything that would tax his arm enough to require icing?* His son, Trey, and my son were good friends, and Trey was a very good pitcher. I mean *extremely* good. His father knew it and was taking advantage of it. When you walked into their backyard, it looked like the training facility for an MLB team. There was a batting machine, a pitching machine, cages, nets, and every other type of baseball training equipment money could buy. My friend and his son were out there constantly, year-round, sharpening Trey's skills and tweaking his technique—that was until the summer of Trey's junior year in high school, when he walked away from the game and told his dad he never wanted to play again. With pro and college scouts banging on his door, he had finally had enough. I asked Trey one day why he didn't want to play professional baseball, and he told me, "I've been playing professional baseball since I was five. I am so done."

When I played football in high school, I played against a couple of guys who eventually went on to play in the NFL, and there was simply something different about them. For instance, when you tried to tackle them, it was like running into an oncoming freight train. They were truly different from the rest of us. Pro coaches and scouts will tell you that a pro athlete is born a pro athlete. They were always the most coordinated, most competitive, and most talented kid at every level. A little pro doesn't need to focus on their bat skills at the age of seven. Let them play whatever, whenever, because their natural skill, physique, and work ethic will eventually shine through and win out. Most experts in the know will tell you that professional athletes are born, not created.

Every Other Aspect of Life Takes a Backseat

One set of parents told me recently that to afford the three thousand dollars it was going to take to pay for their preteen son's baseball trip to several cities on the East Coast, they were going to have to cancel their planned family vacation to Disney World. When I asked how their two young daughters (ages seven and nine) felt about that, the dad quickly said, "Oh, they're all for it. They couldn't be more excited for their brother." Really? Getting a phone call from their parents in Fort Lauderdale telling them that their brother's team came in fifth place in a baseball tournament is just as thrilling and memorable as a trip to the Magic Kingdom?

If every other facet of your family's life takes a backseat to children's sports, then the push is out of control in your family. If a soccer game is scheduled on a Sunday morning, without hesitation, you make sure your kid makes it to the game. If a basketball tournament is scheduled on the same weekend as the grandparents' fiftieth wedding anniversary, then I'm sure Granny and Pops will understand. You scrape every penny together to make sure you have enough money for the traveling lacrosse team, but you can't seem to find any money at all for the yearly missions offering. Yes, your priorities are clear. And what really matters in your family is made clear to your kids.

Do You Care More than Your Child?

Hey, while I'm on a roll here, let me add one last thing that's a surefire indicator that the push is full-blown in your home. If you step back for a moment of reflection and discover that your child's sports career is more important to you than to them—bingo! That's why it's called *the push* and not *the follow*. Are you the one taking notes on everything the coach is saying? Are you the one who pushes for additional practice away from the team? Are you the one who is most upset after a loss? Are you the one bad-mouthing the coach in the car after the game? Are you the one talking about the sport nonstop? Are you the one meticulously dissecting the game when it's over? If you answered yes to any of these questions, take a step back, get a grip, and then get a life. Let your kid be a kid.

According to a *Washington Post* article from October 2015:

Amanda Visek, an exercise science professor at George Washington University, recently surveyed nearly 150 children about what they found fun about sports. (Her sample included kids who play travel and recreational sports.) The kids identified 81 factors contributing to their happiness.

Number 48: winning.

Also low on the list: playing in tournaments, cool uniforms and expensive equipment. High on the list: positive team dynamics, trying hard, positive coaching and learning.

Whenever Visek presents her findings to win-hungry parents and coaches, there is a lot of pushback. "They don't want to believe it," she said.

Yet the No. 1 reason why kids quit sports is that it's no longer fun.[2]

When something gets between you and God, it is considered an idol. An idol is anything that takes God's place of priority in your life or the life of your family. So we have to ask ourselves, *Has my kid's involvement in sports become too important? Has it caused me to sin against God? Is it emphasized more than anything else in my life, or does it bring me more joy than anything else?* If the answer is yes, then it's time to heed the words of Paul, who implored believers to "flee from idolatry" (1 Cor. 10:14). Our lives have no room for idols. What's that old saying? "If Christ is not Lord of all, He's not Lord at all."

Why We Push

I have never confronted a parent about overemphasizing sports who then responded, "Yep, you're right. Guilty as charged. My bad. Wow, that was really dumb. Thank you for being God's instrument of correction in my life. I was so wrapped up in the game that I couldn't see the forest for the trees. I shall now go and sin no more." No, because if they are pushing, then they will fight you on whether they are pushing. If they are pushing, then there is undoubtedly a reason for it. They'll tell you the reason is that their kid has elite talent or loves it so much that they are only following the kid's wishes.

But there is more to it than that.

When people not wrapped up by the push observe these families who are, many are astonished. They are blown away by the huge importance placed on the child's sport, the amount of money spent on the sport, and the vast emotional energy the sport requires (often from the entire family). And when asked why they have succumbed to the all-consuming fixation on the little champ's cheerleading, the parent will say, "Because I love my child, and I'd do anything for them." Yes, they do love their kid very much. No more, I'd remind you, than any parent not consumed with their child's involvement in sports, but they do love them.

However, if you're motivated by love and would do anything for your child, why show this profound love and devotion only in this area? Why not demonstrate that same intense commitment to something else that is undeniably important in their life, like their walk with Christ? Yes, you cart them to Sunday school, but do you find special in-depth Bible studies for them to participate in several times a week? Do you work with them on how to share their testimony with friends for hours and hours until they have it just right? Nutrition is also important for a child, but do you focus with the same focused vigilance in regard to what will best fuel their body?

The answer is, of course, no. Sports win parents' hearts, while these other noble pursuits do not, for many reasons, but let's focus on what I believe is the primary one. Youth sports involve performing in front of a crowd. And with performance in front of a crowd comes the incredibly personal emotions of recognition, acceptance, adulation, scorn, embarrassment, and even perceived judgment. And I'm not talking about the child experiencing these emotions; it's the parent. Many parents assume responsibility for their kid's athletic performance, natural ability, and skill level. Many parents' hearts are filled with pride when their little fella hits a home run; they also feel deep, personal hurt when he strikes out . . . again. A parent's emotional well-being rises and falls according to how their child performs *in front of the crowd*. So in essence, the parent dances like a puppet on the end of the strings being pulled by their twelve-year-old every time he takes the field.

The word to describe this phenomenon is *vicarious*. Many of us have heard this word in church when the preacher talks about Jesus's vicarious death on the cross. In that context, it refers to Jesus dying for us, taking our place on the cross. In the context of youth sports, it refers to parents living their lives through the lives of their children. The parent feels pride and self-importance when the child wins, and dejection and depression when the child loses. This is why the parent does not care as much about how the child performs at their after-school job or how they rank in their current video game. The parent has no public investment in those "performances," but when the stands are full and winning is on the line, oh, they definitely care. They care a great deal. In fact, some parents care so much that they publicly cuss out volunteer umpires, start fistfights in the stands with other parents, get ejected from games for un-sportsmanlike conduct, or demean, reject, and humiliate their child for a bad performance. Why does a grown-up act more like a child than the actual child? Because that parent's sense of self-worth is intimately tied to their child's athletic performance.

The Clear Warning Sign That a Parent Is Pushing

Okay, so how do you know if you're in the push? Of course, you care about how your kid performs. Of course, you want them to win and are sad for them when they lose. You're a parent, not an emotionless robot!

So here's the litmus test for how to tell if you have slipped the sure bonds of reason and taken up residence in "out-of-balanceville." Do you respond to your child in anger based on their athletic performance? Do you talk to them sternly after they have made several mistakes on the field? Do you scold them for not doing what you spent so much time practicing at home? Do you raise your voice at your child when they're not putting forth the effort you expect?

Every other emotion is certainly understandable, but not anger. Anger at your child for their performance on a ball field is . . . wait for it . . . *never justified*. Okay, for some of you, I realize that it's difficult to keep reading because your hands are shaking and your eyes are crossed in anger after having read that you might have an anger problem. I'm sure that in your present state the irony most likely has been lost.

And we're not just talking about the kid who may have just blown his college scholarship due to a bad performance. The parent-to-player anger cycle begins much, much earlier. How many times have you seen a parent get mad when their six-year-old is not paying attention out on the baseball field? They're usually sitting directly behind home plate, screaming, "What are you doing, Sylvester? Stop playing with the stupid dandelions and get your head in the game! How many times do I have to tell you?" And to show the idiocy of this type of behavior, Tom Farrey, author of the great book *Game On,* states, "Scholars who have studied child development have found that most children only begin around age 8 to develop the cognitive and social abilities necessary to understand the complex relationships in competitive, action-oriented team sports."[3] So every day we see parents angrily yelling at their young kids to do something that they are not cognitively capable of doing. It would be like asking the obese, out-of-shape, blow-hard dad who sits behind home plate yelling at his kid to run a hundred-meter dash in less than ten seconds. We could yell at him all day long, but he would not be capable of meeting our demands. We could embarrass him in front of all his friends and a crowd full of strangers, but he still would not be able to do it.

Keep in mind that anger is a secondary emotion. That means anger is the result of our trying to cope with another emotion. Anger is never our first response. It is our reaction to the first emotion we feel. If we could identify the primary emotion for most of these parents, it would be embarrassment, disappointment, or frustration. By the way, did you notice that all these emotions are self-centered? The parent's own self-worth has taken a hit, and anger is the by-product. Anger is triggered when a parent's personal sense of success and achievement is closely wrapped up in a child's athletic performance, when that Little League game means a lot to that parent personally. You can see why so many parents get confused as to what rational priorities are at that moment.

Hopefully you can see that anger is the definitive sign that you are taking your child's sporting life too personally. Their batting average, the number of tackles they have, whether they missed too many serves in the tennis match—none of those things are about you. So encourage them all day long, help them with their game till the cows come home, but you can never justify expressing anger about your child's sports performance.

Three Steps to Exit the Push

1. Define success. What does success mean to you and to those in your family? Well, for believing parents, the Bible is full of instruction on how we should define success, and it is never the same way the world defines it. The general theme of the New Testament is that the first shall lead the league in hitting, right? No, the first *shall be last*. What a huge contrast to our idea of success! In fact, Jesus went on to say, "Whoever wants to be my disciple must deny themselves and take up their cross and follow me. For whoever wants to save their life will lose it, but whoever loses their life for me will find it. What good will it be for someone to gain the whole world, yet forfeit their soul? Or what can anyone give in exchange for their soul?" (Matt. 16:24–26). You see, we can't let our kids think their success or our approval is based on their game stats or MVP medals. Are they trying hard? Are they good friends with the other kids on the team? Are they being a light in a dark place? Are they encouraging to the other players and respectful to the coach? These are the important things. These are what make them a tremendous success in the eyes of the only One who matters.

2. Let your child lead. Let them play the sports *they* want to play—and not all of them at once. Many parents say that it's important for their child to play one sport in

201

particular. Just make sure it's one they're excited about playing. And space out your child's athletic commitments so that they always have a good chunk of the year reserved to simply play and be a child. Encourage, cheer, reassure, comfort, and motivate. Remember that we are to be to our children as God is to us, and I can assure you that God does not yell at you when you strike out in life. He picks you up, tells you He believes in you, and cheers you on the next time you're at the plate.

3. Encourage your child to try hard, work hard, practice hard, and play hard. Why? Not only to win, which is, of course, important, but also because we honor Christ in our hard work, and many times winning gives us a platform through which God can use us to reach others. As Paul writes in Colossians 3:23, "Whatever you do, work at it with all your heart, as working for the Lord, not for human masters." So, parents, encourage your children to practice hard and lift those weights in the off-season, not simply to win a district title, but to do them as if they're doing them specifically for the Lord. It should never be about the roar of the crowd or perceived success in the eyes of friends and family. I'll close this section again with the words of Paul: "Am I now trying to win the approval of human beings, or of God? Or am I trying to please people? If I were still trying to please people, I would not be a servant of Christ" (Gal. 1:10).

We Love Sports

We also want to add that both of us, Jimmy and George, love sports. We both played sports, and all our kids played sports. One of us even got inducted into his school's sports hall of fame for playing the sport he loved. What we want to say is that we don't want you to reject this chapter thinking it was based on a couple of nerds enacting a personal vendetta against involvement in sports. Nothing could be further from the truth. Only the *overemphasis* on sports is under the magnifying glass.

What do you think Paul meant in 2 Corinthians 11:14 when he said Satan himself "masquerades as an angel of light"? Yes, we should not fool ourselves into thinking that Satan is ugly and evil looking. No, he is appealing and attractive, as well as fun and exciting. Sort of like the role that sports can play in a family. Sports are not a bad thing in and of themselves. In fact, sports can provide many things that are essential to our children's upbringing. Kids learn perseverance, courage, toughness, and teamwork through sports. But Satan takes good things and morphs them into destructive things. Our kids' involvement in sports is wonderful. In fact, I think all kids would benefit from team sports. Sports are great . . . until they aren't. Until the entire family has been sucked into the push.

Just think about it. My firsthand observation of thousands of cases leaves no doubt in my mind that most Christian families in America put more money toward their children's involvement in sports, music, and academics than they do into the kingdom of God through the tithe. How would the church be transformed if all those monies, which God has enabled us to make, were directed toward Him and His work, as opposed to traveling select teams? And how would the church be transformed if we took just one-tenth of the time and energy we focus on our kids' sports careers and instead directed that time and energy toward helping the poor and sharing His good news in places where people haven't heard it. Pardon me for borrowing a sports metaphor, but we've taken our eyes off the ball, people! Satan has thrown us a wicked slider, and so far, we have swung and missed.

One Additional Note

Before we leave this topic, let us also say, without any reservations, that your child is also never going to attend Harvard. It simply isn't going to happen. Fewer than .06 percent of all high school graduates do, so the odds of your child walking those hallowed halls are not in your favor. So the same misplaced priorities we have described in regard to athletics could be said about academics as well.

Oh yes, the push is alive and well when it comes to a child's schoolwork. How prideful are we when we are able to tell friends and family that our kid made it into this prestigious private grade school or onto the honor roll or into the National Honor Society? In fact, we humbly say they are simply a chip off the old block. So if you have a little bookworm instead of a little athlete, don't think you're immune from this destructive parental pitfall.

Five Practical Changes You Can Make Today

1. Get together as husband and wife to discuss and decide what success means for your child, then set about encouraging that success in them. Reinforce it as you encourage them toward that goal.

2. Take a deep personal assessment of your attitude and actions concerning your child in sports. Does their "success" on the field mean too much to you? Are you taking it too seriously? What impact is your attitude having on your child? Are you making sports more of an arduous task than a fun game?

3. Okay, you knew this was coming. Do you get angry? Be honest. Do you yell at the coach, officials, fans, or your child in anger? Do you sulk after a bad game? Does your child know how upset you are at their performance? Apologize to your child for how you have messed this up and turn the frown upside down! Begin today with words of encouragement and affirmation toward your child.

4. Begin letting your child lead when it comes to determining the specifics regarding their participation in sports. For example, what sport interests them or what sports do they think they may be good at? Let them drive this train, and let them know you are willing to support them for as long as the ride continues.

5. Let your child know you love them no matter what. You love them when they play well and when they mess up. You love them when they make the all-star team and when they get cut from the squad. Your love for them has nothing to do whatsoever with their performance, because it transcends anything they could ever achieve or merit.

12

Consistent Application Will Enhance Your Parenting Experience

A few years ago, I conducted an unusual study on parenting. We identified people in their twenties who were what we deemed to be "spiritual champions." That is, they loved Jesus Christ, had embraced a lifestyle in which their relationship with Him and their commitment to obeying God's commands were paramount, and they integrated their faith into every dimension of their lives. These were quality people: good citizens, good employees, good spouses and parents, good Christians, and good friends. It's what we used to call the "all-American person" before we became so politically correct and hypersensitive. Once we identified a national sample of twentysomethings who fit the profile, we did extensive interviews with them to find out what they believed their parents had done to enable them to become such commendable people. The results were eye-opening.

But the second crucial portion of that project entailed interviewing the parents of those exemplary young adults. Most of the parents were still living, so we had a large sample of the people who had done the hard work of raising those children to become model citizens and Christians. While the parents did not always confirm the conclusions their children had drawn about their parenting techniques, the similarities were startling—and gave us confidence that the information collected from the two groups was a reliable estimation of what courses of action had produced such stellar human beings.

One of the most valuable questions I asked both groups was perhaps the most obvious: What single most important thing did the parents do to boost the likelihood that the children would become outstanding human beings? The response we received, from parents and children alike, was one of the most consensual replies to any question in the study. They told us that the most important parenting quality of all was *consistency*.

Unless you jumped to the last chapter to see whodunit, you've been exposed to many insights drawn from research and reality about becoming a fearless parent. But unless you are able to incorporate consistency into your parenting skill set, chances are you will undermine your effectiveness. When you apply your parenting principles with consistency, you send the message to your children that you are qualified, reliable, responsible, and trustworthy. Instead of constantly probing to find the soft spots in your parenting philosophy, they will be more likely to invest that energy in a more productive outcome.

Think about the effect of consistent behavior. When you lay down the law and unerringly back it up, you eliminate your children's questions about whether you mean what you say, whether you will support what you say, and whether your view is important to you. Children seek predictability and routine they can follow because those conditions provide them with a greater sense of safety and security. Once they are confident that you really mean it, and your actions reinforce your words and expectations, they are more likely to create their own habits and routines built on the principles you have consistently championed. When you parent them in a predictable manner, they are more likely to respond with predictable behavior.

Think about the path to fearless parenting. It contains a number of components you can master more quickly than you imagine, especially if you are committed to applying those elements with consistency. Let's consider what that might look like by reviewing each of the fearless practices.

Consistent Courage

Embracing and embodying the Christian faith as a parent destroys fear in our lives. Because the Christian faith is laid out for us in the Bible, and that faith is internally consistent, the more we adopt those principles and apply them, the more consistent we can be in our parenting efforts. That will pay mighty dividends on multiple fronts: spiritual, relational, behavioral, and emotional.

When you strip all else away, fearless parenting is really about righteousness. God's Word provides a practical understanding of righteous thinking and behavior, and it is that very approach to life that enables us to parent our youngsters without worries about outcomes or criticism. Because we trust in the power of God, by His Holy Spirit, to work through us when we are seeking to follow His will and do things His way, the ultimate results are truly up to Him. By following His ways, we can also expect His approval. What, then, would we fear? Nothing. And by endlessly going back to His Word to consider how to carry out His will and His ways, we operate in a consistent manner.

In the end, we know Christianity calls us to love God and people. If you can focus your mind and heart on consistently demonstrating care, compassion, understanding, truth, sacrifice, and acceptance toward others, your children will get caught up in that spirit and imitate it in their own lives. What better attribute could you model for them than godly love? The people who consistently have done so—heroes like Mother Teresa, Billy Graham, and John Paul II—have become giants in history because of their unwavering ability to love. They were not overwhelmed by fear, regardless of their circumstances. You can adopt the same kind of consistency in how you raise your children—and achieve the same type of pleasing results and satisfaction.

Consistent Belief

Children are searching for meaning, purpose, direction, and truth. It is our role as parents to show them the way. We must help them grow beyond a one-dimensional faith, making sure they know what they believe by fortifying that knowledge with understanding—that is, helping them to grasp why they believe those things. That is the role of apologetics, a love of which may be best developed through their family experience.

Nothing is better than showing them that you too are devoted to knowing the what and why of your faith by regularly and openly studying the Bible. How much easier is it to ask them to buy into God's Word in all its fullness when they see you setting the example?

And they best learn how to defend the faith by watching you doing that very thing in conversation—without being rude, aggressive, argumentative, or defensive—with those who are not biblically literate or even friendly toward Christianity. Evangelism done well looks easy, but it may not be as easy as it appears. All the great evangelizers I have met—from Billy Graham to pastors and believers whose names are unknown to the masses—spend time studying the Bible in preparation for questions others might pose. Once again, if your life reflects the importance of knowing why you believe key precepts of the faith, that preparation is more likely to be contagious within your family.

Consistently in Charge

Sure, the idea of democratic parenting is popular—but it is neither biblical nor effective. God ordained the parents to be in charge of their children and responsible for their development. Take the role seriously. Master it. Never apologize for it. Own it.

There is no such thing as arm's-length parenting. To influence your children, get involved in their lives at a granular level. Your forms of participation will vary as they grow, but your intensity of engagement in their development should never wane. Be consistently and predictably immersed in their lives without smothering them.

In the midst of that involvement, you get to call a lot of the shots. For instance, it is your job as the parent to identify appropriate life priorities for your children. You cannot make a child accept and love Jesus, but you can provide them with opportunities to do so. Just as important, you can facilitate them in embracing those opportunities and experiences through your own life choices. Only one out of every eight Christians in the United States says their faith is their top priority in life. Are you that one person out of every eight? Only one out of every ten adults has a biblical worldview. Are you that one in ten? Just one out of every twenty churchgoing Christians tithes. Is that you? Two out of every three born-again adults fail to share their faith in Christ with nonbelievers in a typical year. Are you the one who does share the good news? Few parents discuss their church experiences with their children. Do you?

You can talk about priorities until you're blue in the face, but when your children watch you do these things week after week, year after year, they absorb the lesson at a deeper level. The consistency of your behavior will speak louder than your words.

Stand-Out Kids

Have you ever noticed that parents who stand out in the crowd often have children who do the same when they become of age? It's not by accident. I don't even think it has much to do with the gene pool. It's because they spent their formative years observing the adults they knew best and respected the most—and those adults happened to stand out. They discovered the pathway by watching their mom or dad be a person who other people remembered, imitated, or admired.

Every Christian is called to be noticeable in the crowd in a positive way. How do you stand out? Is it by the way you handle adversity and hardship? Is it through the sacrifices you make for the good of others? Is it because you allowed God to break you so He could use you in more substantial ways? Is it because of the wisdom you express with compassion and care? You become a standout not because of a one-time experience, but because you consistently demonstrate your uniqueness in Christ. Do your children have the privilege of seeing that quality in action? Do you give them the freedom to develop the uniqueness that God has entrusted to them?

Consistent Caring

We were made to be in relationship with God and other people, and to love them as best we can. A dynamic relationship demands time, energy, and effort. If you bring a child into the world, be ready to change your lifestyle to accommodate the needs of that child—for the next two decades! Relationships have no shortcuts. Consistency is the name of the game in any solid, lasting relationship.

Investing in listening to your children will no doubt wear you out; it will also lay a strong and permanent foundation for your bond with them. The temptation is to listen when you have nothing better to do or when you have an interest in what they're saying or when you have ignored them for so long that you sense their disillusionment with you. Certainly, you should listen to them during those times. But the real test of a parent is the willingness to truly listen to them when you're juggling more than you can handle, when they chatter on about things you don't understand or don't care about, or when you are too tired to focus on their childish nonsense. Certainly, you should listen to them during those times too.

Being fully present when you are in their company is difficult but necessary. Such investment will enable you to build the trust that facilitates their goals, shapes their priorities, and maximizes their potential. They know when an authority figure simply fades in and out of the picture according to that person's private agenda. But a parent who has prioritized their child and is able to build a deeper relationship by being physically, emotionally, and intellectually present more often than not wins over that young life—for life. Anyone can bounce in and out of their life. Only one who truly loves them will consistently connect with them on multiple levels. (We told you this parenting stuff is tough . . .)

Consistently under Control

The tenor of your relationships with your children also matters. In addition to the consistency of your presence in their lives, they are responsive to the consistency of your commitment to responding in a loving way. Every one of us who has raised children can recall times when we wanted to put them up for instant adoption because they were so irritating or disrespectful or whatever. That's understandable, but it's neither productive nor appropriate.

As an inveterate people watcher, I sometimes marvel at the self-control some parents display when their children go over the edge. Fearless parents somehow develop the capacity not to overreact. Those with whom I have talked often say things like, "Oh, I just prayed for patience and strength"—a comment that may seem a little trite to some but is more accurate than I initially imagined. Rather than revert to the use of guilt, shame, rage, or anger to manipulate the child during the tense moment, these parents are able to suppress a base response in favor of praying, reflecting, and identifying the root cause of the issue.

Are you able to respond with grace and gentleness in stressful moments? Can you dig deep to render acceptance, forgiveness, or understanding? These kinds of reactions, when provided on a consistent basis, make for a fearless and influential parent. But you cannot muster these qualities alone, so invite God into your challenge.

Consistent Contentment

Modern youth culture prods our children to seek material goods they are not entitled to. It subconsciously encourages them to judge others according to wealth and possessions. It fans the flames of material desire and prestigious relationships. And that culture denies that it promotes such things.

But what about us adults? Are we really any different, or are we simply more sophisticated in our quest for comfort and superiority?

You probably know someone who believes they deserve a better title, more vacation time, a higher salary, or a better benefit package than others because they feel they are worth it. Maybe you live in a neighborhood where people drive upscale vehicles they cannot afford but justify it by saying they deserve the best. Perhaps some of your colleagues constantly wear new brand-name clothing even though it is neither necessary nor within their budget to do so.

Your children see these life choices and assume they are viable decisions. You are called, as a parent, to be the antidote to the mind-set of entitlement. Your routine can prove that hard work does not have to end in profligate spending patterns. Your response to other people can teach how our thoughts about others are not based on how they look, what they own, or where they live. Your emphasis on godly purpose, biblical obedience, and joy in living a life for God can rearrange your children's thinking in ways that nothing else in our society can.

Whether or not you are upscale, the bottom line is that everything you have is God's. You are simply His resource manager. Do your choices illustrate for your children the difference between needs and wants? Are your life choices and responses consistent enough to communicate that there is an alternative to the world's way of measuring value and success?

Media Consistency

In a culture totally dependent on technology and electronics, it is not easy to set and maintain boundaries for our children unless we are willing to abide by those same or similar limitations. My research among the parents who raised the "all-American kids" revealed that these parents took media management seriously. Their basic strategy was to monitor, mediate, and minimize their children's media use. That required them to know what content their kids were exposed to, to place and enforce reasonable restrictions on such content, and to discuss the messages of that content with their children, with the goal of helping them develop the ability to self-regulate media intake. But here's the kicker: those parents had to live with similar restrictions.

In some cases, that means providing a substitute for media-driven means of personal acceptance. Instead of posting content designed to generate "likes" on Facebook or retweets on Twitter, perhaps there needs to be a greater emphasis within the home on family or other types of personal relationships and acceptance. Whatever the solution is, you cannot preach about the evils of media obsession if you are constantly texting or playing games on your smartphone or surfing the internet at all hours of the day and night or sending the kids out of the room when your R-rated movie comes on the television. What's good for a young person is most likely good for the old person as well. Send them a consistent message if you want to see them demonstrate consistent behavior.

Making the Most of the Time You Have

I'm a fan of the ancient truism that you're only a child once. What a shame it is when we rush kids to become adults—or even allow them to be rushed into "premature maturity" by the world. Hey, we've been experiencing adulthood for years. What's the hurry, right? Our challenge is to assist them in growing up at the right speed for them, not at the speed a consumption-driven, self-serving world desires. A fearless parent has the wisdom and the courage to fight off the world to allow their child to enjoy the developmental process and to experience it in the most noble and irreproachable way possible. The more ingrained that commitment is within you, the more consistently you will be able to help your child blossom into the person God made them to be.

Notes

Chapter 1 The Need for Fearless Parents

1. "US Debt to Reach $50 Trillion," *World News Daily*, December 7, 2009, http://www.wnd.com/2009/12/118239/.

Chapter 4 Taking Charge of Our Children's Spiritual Growth

1. George Barna, *Transforming Children into Spiritual Champions* (Grand Rapids: Baker Books, 2003).

2. George Barna and David Kinnaman, "Five Reasons Millennials Stay Connected to the Church," Barna Group, September 17, 2013, https://www.barna.com /research/5-reasons-millennials-stay-connected-to-church/#.

3. Ken Ham and Britt Beemer, *Already Gone: Why Your Kids Will Quit Church and What You Can Do to Stop It* (Green Forest, AR: Master Books, 2009), 22.

4. Frank Viola and George Barna, *Pagan Christianity? Exploring the Roots of Our Church Practices* (Carol Stream, IL: Tyndale, 2002), 109.

5. James Edward Stroud, *The Knights Templar and the Protestant Reformation* (Maitland, FL: Xulon Press, 2011).

6. Marcus Yoars, "'Ragamuffin Gospel' Author Brennan Manning Dies," Charisma News, April 13, 2013, http://www.charismanews.com/us/39076-ragamuff in-author-brennan-manning-dies.

Chapter 5 Our Children Are Called to Stand Out

1. Data from a national survey of parents of children under eighteen, conducted by the American Culture & Faith Institute, Woodside, CA, June 2015, among 350 randomly selected Christian parents.

2. David Platt, *Radical: Taking Back Your Faith from the American Dream* (Portland, OR: Multnomah, 2010), 6.

Chapter 6 Prioritize Family Relationships

1. W. Oscar Thompson, *Concentric Circles of Concern: Seven Stages for Making Disciples* (Nashville: Broadman & Holman, 1999).

2. George Barna, *Revolutionary Parenting: What Research Shows Really Works* (Wheaton: Tyndale, 2007).

3. "Time with Parents Key for Adolescents," Population Reference Bureau, April 2015, http://www.prb.org/Publications/Articles/2015/parental-time.aspx; Brigid Schulte, "Making Time for Kids? Study Shows Quality Trumps Quantity," *Washington Post*, March 28, 2015, https://www.washingtonpost.com/local/making-time-for-kids-study-says-quality-trumps-quantity/2015/03/28/10813192-d378-11e4-8fce-3941fc548f1c_story.html?utm_term=.8b577f08ae05; Kim Parker and Wendy Wang, "Modern Parenthood," Pew Research Center, March 14, 2013, http://www.pewsocialtrends.org/2013/03/14/modern-parenthood-roles-of-moms-and-dads-converge-as-they-balance-work-and-family/; Sharon Jayson, "Men vs. Women: How Much Time Spent on Kids, Jobs, Chores," *USA Today*, March 14, 2013, http://www.usatoday.com/story/news/nation/2013/03/14/men-women-work-time/1983271/.

Chapter 7 Reject Destructive Parental Behaviors: Anger, Guilt, and Shame

1. Brennan Manning, *The Ragamuffin Gospel: Good News for the Bedraggled, Beat-Up, and Burnt Out* (Colorado Springs: Multnomah, 2005), 117.

2. Steve Weinberg, "Address at the Conference on Cosmic Design, American Association for the Advancement of Science," Washington, DC, April 1999.

Chapter 8 Reject Materialistic Entitlement

1. See Matthew 19:24; Mark 10:25; Luke 18:25.

2. David Goetz, *Death by Suburb: How to Keep the Suburbs from Killing Your Soul* (San Francisco: HarperOne, 2006), 9.

3. Frank Harris, *Oscar Wilde, His Life and Confessions* (Ware, Hertfordshire, UK: Wordsworth Editions, 2007), 268.

4. Craig Groeschel, *The Christian Atheist: Believing in God but Living as If He Doesn't* (Grand Rapids: Zondervan, 2010), 165.

5. C. S. Lewis, *God in the Dock: Essays on Theology and Ethics* (Grand Rapids: Eerdmans, 1970), 48.

6. Simon Sinek, "How to Get People to Follow You," *Inside Quest* (video blog), accessed January 24, 2017, http://www.insidequest.com/episode/simon-sinek/.

Chapter 9 Rethinking Social Media and Smartphone Use

1. Sinek, "How to Get People to Follow You."

2. Amanda Lenhart, "Teens, Social Media, and Technology Overview 2015," Pew Research Center, April 9, 2015, http://www.pewinternet.org/2015/04/09/teens-social-media-technology-2015/.

3. Ibid.

4. American Culture & Faith Institute, Woodside, CA, 2015, Right View 18, N=350 parents of children under age eighteen.

5. Dara Kerr, "Smartphones Commandeer 70 Percent of Teen Market," c/net, October 29, 2013, https://www.cnet.com/news/smartphones-commandeer-70-percent-of-teen-market/.

6. Common Sense Media, *Common Sense Census: Media Use by Tweens and Teens*, 2015, https://www.commonsensemedia.org/sites/default/files/uploads/research/census_executivesummary.pdf.

7. Albert Mehrabian, *Silent Messages: Implicit Communication of Emotions and Attitudes*, 2nd ed. (Boston: Wadsworth Publishing, 1980).

Chapter 10 The Porn-Again Child

1. "Teens and Young Adults Use Porn More than Anyone Else," Barna Group, January 28, 2016, https://barna.org/research/culture-media/research-release/teens-young-adults-use-porn-more-than-anyone-else; David Kinnaman, "The Porn Phenomenon," Barna Group, January 19, 2016, https://www.barna.org/blog/culture-media/david-kinnaman/the-porn-phenomenon.

2. Ibid.

3. Ibid.

4. Ibid.

5. Martin J. Downing Jr., Eric W. Schrimshaw, Roberta Scheinmann, et al., "Sexually Explicit Media Use by Sexual Identity: A Comparative Analysis of Gay, Bisexual, and Heterosexual Men in the United States," *Archives of Sexual Behavior*, October 5, 2016, http://link.springer.com/article/10.1007/s10508-016-0837-9.

6. "American Teens' Sexual and Reproductive Health," Guttmacher Institute, June 2016; Barna Group, YouthPoll, a national survey among 602 randomly sampled teenagers.

Chapter 11 Parental Self-Worth and the Push

1. "Youth Sports Statistics," Statistics Brain, accessed December 16, 2016, http://www.statisticbrain.com/youth-sports-statistics/; Tony Manfred, "Here Are the Odds that Your Kid Becomes a Professional Athlete (Hint: They're Small)," Business Insider, February 10, 2012, http://www.businessinsider.com/odds-college-athletes-become-professionals-2012-2?op=1; "Probability of Competing beyond High School," NCAA, accessed December 17, 2016, http://www.ncaa.org/about/resources/research/probability-competing-beyond-high-school; "Making It to the Pros," unpublished statistical analysis, Metaformation, 2016; "Percentage Chance of Playing NCAA College Sports," College Sports Scholarships, accessed December 17, 2016, http://www.collegesportsscholarships.com/percentage-high-school-athletes-ncaa-college.htm.

2. Michael S. Rosenwald, "Are Parents Ruining Youth Sports? Fewer Kids Play amid Pressure," *Washington Post*, October 4, 2015, https://www.washingtonpost.com/local/are-parents-ruining-youth-sports-fewer-kids-play-amid-pressure/2015/10/04/eb1460dc-686e-11e5-9ef3-fde182507eac_story.html?utm_term=.d4cdf44b5e45.

3. Tom Farrey, *Game On: The All-American Race to Make Champions of Our Children* (New York: ESPN Books, 2008), 98.

George Barna currently serves as the executive director of the American Culture and Faith Institute, conducting research on governance, elections, worldview, and cultural transformation. He is the *New York Times* bestselling and award-winning author of more than fifty books, and his work is frequently cited as an authoritative source by the media. A frequent speaker at ministry conferences around the world, he has been on the faculty at several universities and seminaries. George and his wife, Nancy, have three adopted daughters and two grandchildren and live on the central California coast.

Jimmy Myers was involved in youth ministry in the local church for more than twenty years before making the jump to psychotherapy. A licensed professional counselor, he speaks to youth and their parents at conferences and retreats across the country. In 2001, he founded the Timothy Center, a multicampus Christian counseling practice located in Austin, Texas, that focuses on the needs and issues of adolescents and their families. He has authored, coauthored, and compiled several books and articles for youth and parents, and is assistant professor with the Center for Counseling and Family Studies at Liberty University. Jimmy and his wife, Beth, have three children and five grandchildren and live north of Austin, Texas.

HOW TO CONTACT, FOLLOW, AND RECEIVE
MORE CONTENT FROM JIMMY MYERS

WWW.PAIRADOCSPODCAST.COM

Pairadocs is a unique marriage and parenting podcast that women will love and guys won't want to turn off. You can find the show on iTunes, Google Play, and all other major podcast platforms.

For speaking inquiries, contact The Fedd Agency at www.TheFeddAgency.com

@DocJimmyMyers   @JMyersFam   DocJimmyMyers

How to Follow and Receive More Content from
George Barna

www.GeorgeBarna.com

Visit www.CultureFaith.com for more content
from George Barna, including:

- A free subscription to the research-based, weekly
  newsletter about cultural transformation with the
  American Culture Review

- Special reports based on national research
  conducted through the American Culture & Faith
  Institute